Everyday Situations for Communicating in English

Rebecca Rauff

Rudolph Rau

Illustrations by
James Buckley

National Textbook Company
a division of NTC/CONTEMPORARY PUBLISHING GROUP
Lincolnwood, Illinois USA

For all the people who thought
I would write a book someday;
with special thanks
to Jim, Andy, and Kathleen
for making it possible

R. Rauff

Additional illustrations on pages 8, 46, 66, 78, 104, and 128
by Rebecca Brown

Layout and design by Betty McCasland

ISBN: 0-8442-0676-8

Published by National Textbook Company,
a division of NTC/Contemporary Publishing Group, Inc.,
4255 West Touhy Avenue,
Lincolnwood (Chicago), Illinois 60646-1975 U.S.A.
© 1993 by NTC/Contemporary Publishing Group, Inc.
8 9 0 WKT 9 8 7

Contents

To the Student

Everyday Situations for Communicating in English is your guide to everyday life. It uses big, colorful pictures to show places you *need* to go, like supermarkets and banks, and places you *want* to go, like beaches and amusement parks. Every picture is filled with people doing many different things.

The activities and exercises in this book will help you learn the language you need for everyday life in the United States. You will become more comfortable and fluent in English as you and your classmates talk about the pictures and learn about American customs and lifestyles.

But language isn't just for *talking about* life, it's for *living* life! So **Everyday Situations for Communicating in English** takes you "into" each picture to practice what you would say if you were in that situation. Then the activities in each chapter take you back "out" of the pictures to practice everyday skills such as ordering a meal or mailing a letter.

Everyday Situations for Communicating in English is divided into four thematic units: **Faces of America, Around Town, On the Go,** and **Just for Fun.** The chapters in each unit focus on specific parts of life in the United States that are related to the unit theme.

If you live in the United States, this book will help you to understand and participate in the world around you. If you are studying English in another country, this book will prepare you for future travel or study in the United States. Whatever your reason for studying English, **Everyday Situations for Communicating in English** will let you "see" how Americans really live and help you to learn and practice the language Americans really use.

Unit One
Faces of America

The United States is the fourth largest country in the world. It has more than three and a half million square miles (over nine million square kilometers) of mountains, deserts, beaches, forests, and farmlands. Of course, a country this big is full of different people, places, and lifestyles. But in many ways, life is the same all over the United States.

Unit 1 begins with a look at one historic "entrance" to the United States. **Chapter 1: New York City's Battery Park** takes us to some famous parts of New York City, the first city many people see when they come to the United States.

Chapter 2: A City Street shows a scene from a "typical" large American city. You may be surprised to see how much it looks like other cities all over the world!

Chapter 3: On a Farm shows another side of life in the United States. Not all Americans live in big cities like New York, Chicago, or Los Angeles. Many Americans live in small towns or on farms.

Chapter 4: A Thanksgiving Day Dinner ends this unit with a traditional American Thanksgiving celebration. All across the United States, Americans follow similar customs when they celebrate their national holidays.

Chapter 1
New York City's Battery Park

Warm-Up

❏ Why is New York City famous?

❏ Did you ever go to New York City? If so, what did you see there?

Words to Know

A. Here are the names of some things you can find in and around New York City's Battery Park. Look for them in the picture.

American flag	cannon	sea gull
boat	ferry	statue
bridge	island	Statue of Liberty
camera	ocean	street vendor

B. Here are some other words you can use to talk about the Battery Park area. Study these words and their meanings.

bay   (n) part of an ocean that curves into the land

to board   (v) to get on (a boat)

eagle   (n) a large bird with sharp eyes and strong wings. The eagle is a symbol of the United States.

fort   (n) a strong building made to keep enemies out

immigrant   (n) a person who moves to a new country

to immigrate   (v) to move to a new country

memorial   (n) something that helps people remember an event or a person

monument   (n) a building or statue that helps people remember an important person or event

museum   (n) a place where people can see and learn about art or other interesting things

sight   (n) something that is worth looking at

sightseeing   (n) going to see interesting places

suspension bridge   (n) a bridge that hangs on chains or heavy ropes between two towers

torch   (n) a light or flame for carrying

tourist   (n) a person who is sightseeing

C. Study these words and their meanings. Then look for examples of these objects and activities in the picture.

garbage barge   (n) a boat that carries trash from a city for dumping in another place

kayak   (n) a canoe-like boat for one person

megaphone   (n) a device that makes a person's voice sound louder

terminal   (n) the place where a boat, bus, plane, or train begins and/or ends a trip

tugboat   (n) a small boat that pulls bigger boats

to wait in line   (v) to stand behind other people until it is your turn

Now complete these sentences with words from List B. Change the form of a word if necessary.

1. Many _____ visit New York City every year.

2. Sophie _____ to the United States in 1978.

3. Max and Marta went _____ yesterday. They saw some _____ in the park and visited an art _____ .

Understanding the Picture

1. There are many famous sights in the Battery Park area of New York City. Find these sights in the picture.

    a. the Statue of Liberty
    b. Ellis Island (to the right of Liberty Island)
    c. the Verrazano-Narrows Bridge (at top of picture)
    d. Brooklyn (to the left of the bridge)
    e. Staten Island (to the right of the bridge)

2. Which of these things do you see in the picture?

    a. a fire boat   e. a tugboat
    b. a fort   f. a tow truck
    c. a statue   g. tourists
    d. a fish   h. a fisherman

3. Find someone in the picture who is doing each of these things.

a. buying a balloon
b. walking a dog
c. taking a picture
d. feeding the birds
e. waiting in line
f. waving
g. selling hot dogs
h. listening to music

4. There are many kinds of boats in this picture. Which of these boats can tourists ride in?

a. a garbage barge
b. a Coast Guard boat
c. the Staten Island Ferry
d. a tugboat
e. a kayak
f. a fire boat
g. The Statue of Liberty Ferry

What Do You See?

Study this part of the picture. Then answer the questions.

1. What are the cars doing?

2. What can you buy in this part of Battery Park?

3. What is the family doing by the water?

4. What are the people in the red hats and shirts doing by the ferry terminal?

5. What is the balloon vendor wearing? Why?

What Are They Saying?

The family by the water is talking about the Statue of Liberty. Practice their conversation in groups of three.

FATHER: Look! There's the Statue of Liberty!

CHILD: Wow! It's really big.

MOTHER: It sure is. I read in our guidebook that it's 151 feet tall.

CHILD: I wonder who built it.

FATHER: It was designed by a Frenchman named Frederic Bartholdi, but I don't know who really built it.

MOTHER: France gave it to the United States to celebrate our country's one hundredth birthday.

CHILD: How old is Lady Liberty now?

MOTHER: She's more than a hundred years old—and she's still an important symbol of freedom and opportunity in this country.

CHILD: That's pretty neat! Can we take the ferry over to Liberty Island?

FATHER: Sure. We can even climb up to the statue's crown, if you want to.

CHILD: Great! Let's go!

Now work with your group to change the conversation so that

- The mother read in the guidebook that the statue's torch is 21 feet long, and each hand is about 16 feet long.
- The child asks if they can climb up to the statue's torch.
- The father thinks they can only go up to the crown.
- The child wants to get in line for the ferry now.

Practice your new conversation together.

What Will Happen Next?

Answer these questions in small groups. Then compare your answers with those of the other groups.

1. What will happen to the people who are walking toward the ferry terminal?

2. What will the family to the left of the balloon vendor do next?

3. What will the man in the striped shirt by the hot dog vendor do next?

What Would You Say?

Act out this situation with a partner. Take turns playing parts A and B.

A. You live in New York City. A friend from another country is visiting you. You take your friend to Battery Park to see the Statue of Liberty. You ask if your friend wants to take the ferry over to Liberty Island and climb up to the crown of the statue.

B. You are visiting a friend in New York City. You are very interested in seeing the Statue of Liberty. You ask your friend many questions about the history of the statue. You want to go over to Liberty Island, but you don't want to climb up to the statue's crown.

What Do You See?

Study this part of the picture. Then answer the questions.

1. What is the man with the megaphone doing?

2. What are the people on the ferry doing?

3. What are the sea gulls doing?

4. What are the people doing while they wait in line?

5. What are the children climbing on?

What Are They Saying?

The two women by the ice cream vendor are talking about their plans for the day. Practice their conversation with a partner.

WOMAN 1: Do you want to go over to Ellis Island?

WOMAN 2: I don't know. What can you see there?

WOMAN 1: Oh, it's really interesting! You know, many people who immigrated to the United States in the late 1800s and early 1900s had to stop at Ellis Island before they could go into the country.

WOMAN 2: I know. My grandparents came through Ellis Island in the 1930s.

WOMAN 1: You're not alone. About forty percent of all Americans have relatives who came through Ellis Island. It's a special place for many people.

WOMAN 2: I heard that the island was fixed up and opened for tourists in 1990.

WOMAN 1: Yes. There's a wonderful museum that shows what the immigrants saw and did at Ellis Island.

WOMAN 2: Well, let's go see it. How do we get there?

WOMAN 1: We can take a ferry from here. They leave every half hour. The ferry will stop at Liberty Island, too.

WOMAN 2: Oh, good. Let's go get our tickets!

Now work with your partner to change the conversation so that

- Woman 1 asks her friend what she wants to do today.
- Woman 2 asks what you can see at Ellis Island.
- Woman 1's grandparents came through Ellis Island, too.
- Woman 2 asks if they can take a ferry to Ellis Island.

Practice your new conversation together.

What Will Happen Next?

Answer these questions in small groups. Then compare your answers with those of the other groups.

1. What will happen to the woman on the top level of the ferry?

2. What will happen to the children who are playing on the cannon?

3. What will the man who is feeding the birds do next?

What Would You Say?

Act out this situation in groups of three. Take turns playing parts A, B, and C.

A. You and two friends are in Battery Park. You are talking about what to do today. You want to take the ferry to Liberty Island.

B. You and two friends are in Battery Park. You are talking about what to do. You want to go to Ellis Island.

C. You and two friends arc in Battery Park. You are talking about what to do today. You ask your friends why they want to go to Liberty Island and Ellis Island. You don't know much about these sights.

Let's Practice

Many people take tours of New York City. A bus tour is one way to see many sights easily and quickly. Look at this magazine advertisement for some bus tours offered by the Crown Tour Company.

Beat the Heat on Crown's Cool Buses

Crown Tours, New York's oldest and largest tour company, offers more than 30 tours of the city. All our buses have air conditioning, comfortable seats for 40, and large tinted windows. Our drivers and tour guides are friendly and experienced. Tours leave daily from our convenient bus center in midtown Manhattan.

Here are just a few of the tours we offer:

Tour 1: The Financial District

Sights include the World Trade Center, Wall Street, the New York Stock Exchange, the World Financial Center, and Battery Park.

Options: A. the Staten Island Ferry
B. Liberty Island
C. Ellis Island and Liberty Island

Departures: Monday and Wednesday—9:30 A.M., 2:00 P.M.
Friday and Saturday—9:30 A.M.

Tour 2: Midtown Manhattan

Sights include the United Nations Headquarters, the New York Public Library, the Trump Tower, St. Patrick's Cathedral, Rockefeller Center, and Radio City Music Hall.

Options: A. Central Park
B. the Museum of Modern Art
C. the Empire State Building

Departures: Tuesday and Thursday—10:00 A.M., 3:00 P.M.
Saturday—10:00 A.M., 3:00 P.M., 7:00 P.M.

Tour 3: The Upper West Side

Sights include the Lincoln Center for the Performing Arts, the Metropolitan Opera, the Julliard School of Music, the American Museum of Natural History, and Columbia University.

Option: walking tour of the Lincoln Center

Departures: Monday, Tuesday, and Saturday—9:00 A.M.
Sunday—11:00 A.M.

Prices start at just $10.00 for adults, $5.00 for children under 12. For more information, call 555-7000 and ask for our FREE tour catalog. Or stop by our beautiful new bus center at 714 RANDOLPH STREET, MANHATTAN.

GROUPS WELCOME! Special tours and group prices are available for groups of 20 or more.

LEAVE YOUR CARS AND CARES AT HOME
SEE NEW YORK THE CROWN WAY!

Crown Tours
Serving New York
Since 1937

Understanding the Advertisement

Work with a partner to answer these questions about the advertisement.

1. How many bus tours does Crown Tours offer?

2. How many days a week are the tours available?

3. Where do the tours begin?

4. How much does a Crown bus tour cost?

5. How long has Crown Tours been in business?

6. How can you get more information about Crown's bus tours?

7. What are Crown's buses like?

Choosing a Tour

With your partner, answer these questions about the tours described in the advertisement.

1. Which tour(s) can you take on a Monday?

2. Which tour(s) can you take on a Saturday?

3. Which tour(s) can you take in the afternoon?

4. Which tour(s) can you take in the evening?

5. You want to go to the Museum of Modern Art. Which tour should you take?

6. You want to see the Lincoln Center. Which tour should you take?

7. You want to go to Liberty Island. Which tour should you take?

8. You want to see the World Trade Center. Which tour should you take?

Let's Learn More

Read these paragraphs about New York City.

Battery Park

Battery Park got its name from a **battery** of cannons that once stood in the northern part of the park. The cannons were placed there by the British after they took the city from the Dutch in 1664. The purpose of the cannons was to **defend** the city from its enemies.

Castle Clinton, in the southern part of the park, was built in 1808 to help defend the city. It is now a historical monument, with an **exhibit** for visitors. Another monument in Battery Park is the East Coast Memorial, which **honors** the Americans who died off the East Coast of the United States during World War II. This memorial has a statue of an eagle and eight large pieces of stone.

Ellis Island

From Battery Park, visitors can take a ferry to Ellis Island. From 1892 to 1954, about twelve million immigrants stopped at Ellis Island before entering the United States. Here their health and personal information were checked.

Most of the immigrants passed through Ellis Island in a few hours. Those who needed more **inspection** often had to stay on the island for days or weeks. But only about two percent of the immigrants who came to Ellis Island were sent home.

For almost thirty years, Ellis Island was not used. It reopened as a museum and tourist center in 1990. The museum honors all immigrants to the United States.

Vocabulary Check

Study these words and their meanings.

battery   (n) a group of guns
to defend   (v) to protect someone or something from attack
exhibit   (n) a showing of art or other interesting things
to honor   (v) to show respect for someone or something
inspection   (n) examination; a careful checking

Now choose the best word to complete each sentence.

1. A _____ takes people from Battery Park to Ellis Island. (battery, ferry)

2. Castle Clinton was built to help _____ New York City. (defend, honor)

3. The East Coast Memorial has a _____ of an eagle. (cannon, statue)

4. Between 1892 and 1954, about twelve million _____ passed through Ellis Island. (tourists, immigrants)

5. Today, the museum at Ellis Island has _____ about the immigrants who stopped there. (inspections, exhibits)

Comprehension Check

Complete these sentences about some famous New York City sights.

1. Battery Park

2. Castle Clinton

3. The East Coast Memorial

4. Ellis Island

a. honors Americans who died during World War II.

b. was a place for checking immigrants' health and personal information.

c. was built in 1808.

d. got its name from a group of cannons.

Extension Activity

With your classmates, make a chart that shows the year each student's family came to the United States and the country each family came from. How many of the families came from the same countries? How many came to the United States during the same years? Talk about which student's family traveled the farthest, arrived first, and so on.

Then tell the class or a small group about how, when, and why your family came to the United States. Listen to your classmates and ask questions about their families and experiences.

Chapter 2

A City Street

Warm-Up

❑ What is the biggest city you ever visited or lived in? Do you like that city? Why or why not?

❑ What are some things you can see on a city street?

Words to Know

A. Here are the names of some things you can find on a city street. Look for them in the picture.

bus
cab
cane
crosswalk
curb
delicatessen (deli)
department store
fire hydrant

fountain
hotel
limousine
movie theater
pharmacy
phone booth
police officer
restaurant

sidewalk
store
street musician
street vendor
subway stop
taxi
traffic light
whistle

B. Many activities take place on a city street. Look for examples of these activities in the picture.

to be in a hurry
to cross a street
to direct traffic

to get on/off a bus
to park (a car)
to wait in line

C. Here are more words you can use to talk about the picture. Study these words and their meanings.

blimp   (n) a balloon-like airship
dog guide   (n) a dog that is trained to help a blind person
doorman   (n) someone whose job is to help people at the door of a hotel or apartment building
to hail a taxi   (v) to get a taxi by waving a hand or shouting

hopscotch   (n) a children's game in which players hop in squares drawn on the ground
illegal   (adj) not legal; against the law
intersection   (n) a place where two or more streets cross each other
parking ticket   (n) a paper which says that a car is illegally parked. The owner of the car has to pay money for parking in the wrong place.
scaffold   (n) a platform for workers to stand on high above the ground
traffic   (n) cars, buses, and trucks moving on a street
traffic jam   (n) a place on a street where traffic is stopped or moving very slowly

Now complete these sentences with words from Lists B and C. Change the form of a word if necessary.

1. Sylvia was late for work because of the _____ on 42nd Street.

2. If you leave your car by a fire hydrant, you will get a _____.

3. Stay in the crosswalk when you _____.

4. A police officer is _____ at the _____ of Oak and Elmwood Streets.

Understanding the Picture

1. Which of these businesses do you see on this street?

   a. a pharmacy
   b. a supermarket
   c. a delicatessen
   d. a service station
   e. a movie theater
   f. a hotel
   g. a department store
   h. a bank

   What other businesses do you see on this street?

2. Find the place(s) in the picture where you can do each of these things.

   a. mail a letter
   b. buy a movie ticket
   c. shop for clothes
   d. eat lunch
   e. make a telephone call
   f. get on the subway
   g. listen to music
   h. buy a snack

3. Many people are working on this street. Which of these workers do you see?

a. a mail carrier
b. a construction worker
c. a window washer
d. a police officer
e. a teacher
f. a bus driver
g. an ice cream vendor
h. a doctor

What other workers do you see on this street?

4. There are many ways to travel in a city. Which of these kinds of transportation do you see in this picture?

a. taxi
b. tow truck
c. limousine
d. airplane
e. bus
f. subway
g. skateboard
h. bicycle

What Do You See?

Study this part of the picture. Then answer the questions.

1. What is the man sitting on the ground doing? What is in his hat?

2. Why does the man with the orange cap have a cane and a dog? What is the dog's job?

3. What is the mail carrier doing?

4. What is the man in the brown sweater doing by the phone booth?

5. What is the police officer doing?

What Are They Saying?

The woman in the phone booth is talking to her friend. Practice their conversation with a partner.

WOMAN: Cindy! This is Janet.
         I'm so glad you're home.

FRIEND: Hi, Janet. What's going on?

WOMAN: I locked myself out of my apartment.

FRIEND: Oh, no! Where are you?

WOMAN: I'm over in Grandview Park.
         I was going to the pharmacy,
         and I left my keys at home.

FRIEND: Where's your roommate?

WOMAN: She's out of town. She won't be back
         until tomorrow night!

FRIEND: Oh, dear. Can the building
         superintendent let you in?

WOMAN: Yes, but I can't find him right now!

FRIEND: Well, let me come over and get you.
         We can go out for lunch and then look
         for the superintendent.

WOMAN: Okay. Thank you, Cindy.

FRIEND: No problem. Wait for me in front
         of your building. I'll be there
         in about twenty minutes.

Now work with your partner to change the conversation so that

• Janet's roommate is out shopping. Janet doesn't know when she'll be home.
• The building superintendent is out of town today.
• Cindy invites Janet to stay at her apartment until her roommate gets home.
• Janet will take the subway to Cindy's apartment.

Practice your new conversation together.

What Will Happen Next?

Answer these questions in small groups. Then compare your answers with those of the other groups.

1. What will the young man with the map do next?

2. What will the mail carrier do next?

3. What will happen to the boy who is leaning out of the orange car?

What Would You Say?

Act out this situation in groups of three. Take turns playing parts A, B, and C.

A. You just got home from school. You can't find your key. You go to a neighbor's house to use the phone.

B. Your neighbor comes over. You let him call his mother at work. You say he can stay until she gets home.

C. You are at work. Your child calls to say he can't find his key. You have a meeting, so you can't come home early. You ask to talk to the neighbor.

What Do You See?

Study this part of the picture. Then answer the questions.

1. What is the police officer doing?

2. Why is the man in the red shirt running across the street?

3. What is the man with the tall hat doing? What is his job?

4. What is the man in the plaid shirt and blue pants doing? How does he feel?

5. How do the young man in the purple pants and the young woman in the yellow pants feel about each other? How can you tell?

What Are They Saying?

The man in the red shirt is talking to the police officer. Practice their conversation with a partner.

MAN: Officer! Wait, officer! That's my car!

POLICE OFFICER: Oh, it is? Then I won't need a tow truck.

MAN: No! I'll move it right away!

POLICE OFFICER: Good. It's illegal to park beside a fire hydrant.

MAN: I know, but there wasn't anywhere else to park. I was only gone for a minute.

POLICE OFFICER: I see. Here's your ticket.

MAN: You're going to give me a ticket?

POLICE OFFICER: That's right. You broke the law.

MAN: But just for a minute!

POLICE OFFICER: Every minute is important when fire fighters need water.

Now work with your partner to change the conversation so that

- The man asks the police officer what is wrong.
- The police officer tells the man his car is next to a fire hydrant.
- The man is surprised.
- The police officer shows him the fire hydrant. It's bright red.
- The man says he didn't see the fire hydrant. He was in a hurry to go to a movie.

Practice your new conversation together.

What Will Happen Next?

Answer these questions in small groups. Then compare your answers with those of the other groups.

1. Where will the couple getting into the limousine go?

2. What will happen to the dog that's by the fire hydrant?

3. What will the man at the movie ticket window do next?

What Would You Say?

Act out this situation with a partner. Take turns playing parts A and B.

A. You are shopping downtown. You leave a store and see a police officer looking at your car. You ask the officer what is wrong. You thought this was a good parking place.

B. You are a police officer. You see a car parked by a no-parking sign. The driver of the car comes back. You give the driver a ticket.

Let's Practice

In order to move around safely in an American city, you must understand and obey the traffic signs you can see on every street and highway. These signs give information and instructions to drivers, bicyclists, and pedestrians (people walking). The shapes and colors of traffic signs tell a lot about their meaning.

Here are some examples:

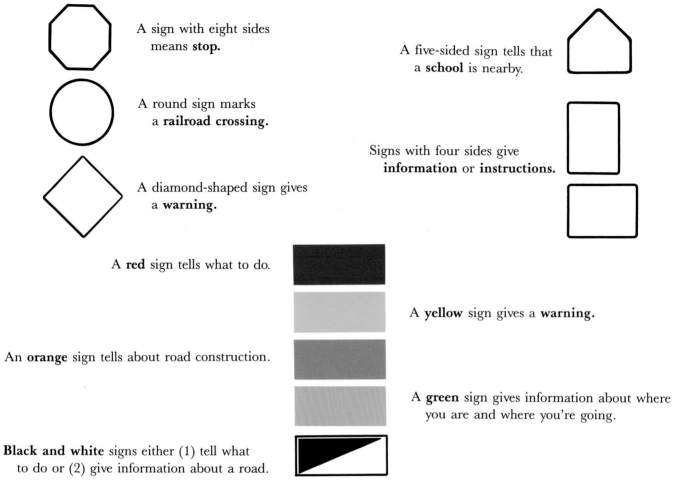

A sign with eight sides means **stop.**

A round sign marks a **railroad crossing.**

A diamond-shaped sign gives a **warning.**

A five-sided sign tells that a **school** is nearby.

Signs with four sides give **information** or **instructions.**

A **red** sign tells what to do.

A **yellow** sign gives a **warning.**

An **orange** sign tells about road construction.

A **green** sign gives information about where you are and where you're going.

Black and white signs either (1) tell what to do or (2) give information about a road.

Study the information above.
Then work in small groups to tell the meaning of each of these signs.

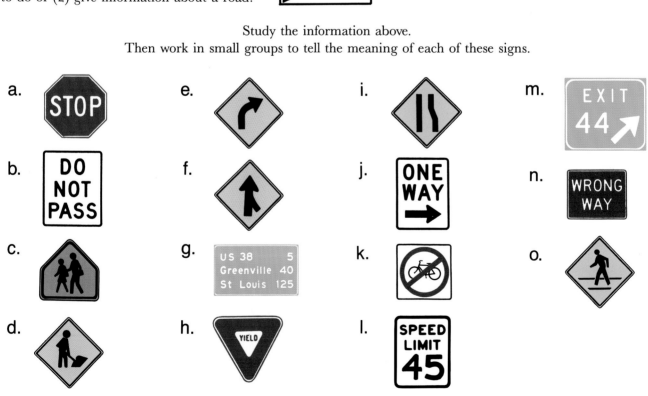

Let's Learn More

Read these paragraphs about U.S. cities.

The United States is an **urban** nation. About seventy-five percent of Americans live in or near a large city. Some people believe that in the future the United States will be filled with "megalopolises": huge urban areas made up of several cities and their **suburbs.**

The United States was not always a nation of cities. In 1790, only five percent of Americans lived in cities. When the Civil War began in 1861, only twenty percent of Americans lived in cities. But in the late 1800s and early 1900s, the United States became **industrialized.** Many people moved from **rural** areas into cities to find jobs. At the same time, many people from other countries came to live and work in U.S. cities. In 1920, for the first time, more than half the nation lived in cities.

Today, America's cities are full of **contrasts.** They are home to thousands of successful businesses, but also to millions of poor and unemployed people. Many U.S. cities are fighting the death of their downtown areas as stores, restaurants, and other businesses move to suburban shopping centers. Crime, traffic jams, pollution, and high prices are a part of life in most American cities. At the same time, U.S. cities offer business opportunities, cultural events, shops, sporting events, and entertainment that **attract** people from all over the country and all over the world.

Vocabulary Check

Study these words and their meanings.

to attract   (v) to make someone want to come nearer
contrasts   (n) big differences
industrialized   (adj) full of highly developed businesses that involve many people, machines, and modern methods
rural   (adj) having to do with the countryside
suburb   (n) a small town or community on the edge of a big city
urban   (adj) having to do with a city or cities

Now find words in the reading that mean the opposite of these words and phrases.

1. urban
2. past
3. less
4. similarities
5. having a job
6. life

Comprehension Check

Answer the questions in complete sentences.

1. Where do most Americans live today? Where did they live two hundred years ago?

2. What is a "megalopolis"?

3. Why did many people move to U.S. cities in the late 1800s and early 1900s?

4. What are some of the problems you will find in an American city?

5. Why do many people like American cities?

Extension Activity

Make a "Welcome to Our City" handbook with your class. The book will be for new students in your class or school. It will have information they need to know about the city you live in or a nearby city.

As a class, make a list of topics to include in your book (for example: public transportation, inexpensive shopping, and good restaurants). Your teacher will help you decide how long the book can be and how many topics you can use. Then work in pairs or small groups to prepare one page of information for each topic.

Exchange pages with another pair or group. Read and talk about each other's work. Do you understand it? Does it answer all your questions about the topic?

Does it include all the important information? Listen to the comments about your page. Then make any necessary changes and rewrite it.

If possible, give copies of all the pages to each student in the class. Read the handbook pages and think about them. Then have a class discussion about the handbook. Is everything explained well? Should you add any information? Work together to make any necessary changes.

Choose a title for your handbook and make a cover for it. Then make several copies of the handbook to give to new students who join your class. Give a few copies to your school principal or counselor, who can give them to other new students at the school.

Chapter 3
On a Farm

Warm-Up

❑ What are some things you can see on a farm? ❑ What does a farmer do?

Words to Know

A. Here are the names of some things you can find on a farm. Look for them in the picture.

barn	field	pickup truck
chicken	garden	pig
cow	goose	pond
duck	hay	scarecrow
egg	hay bale	sheep
farmhouse	hoe	tractor
fence	horse	

B. Here are some other words you can use to talk about a farm. Study these words and their meanings.

feed   (n) food for farm animals
fertilizer   (n) something that helps plants grow
to harvest   (v) to gather in grain, fruits, or vegetables
livestock   (n) farm animals
to milk   (v) to take milk from a female animal's udder
orchard   (n) a place where fruit trees grow
pasture   (n) an area of grass for animals to eat
seed   (n) the part of a plant that can be used to grow new plants
soil   (n) earth; dirt

C. Study these words and their meanings. Then look for examples of these objects and activities in the picture.

to chase   (v) to run after someone or something
chicken coop   (n) a small building where chickens live
conveyor belt   (n) a machine with a moving belt that carries things from one place to another
to feed   (v) to give food to
hayloft   (n) a place for hay on the top level of a barn
to lay an egg   (v) to make an egg and release it from one's body
milking machine   (n) a machine that takes milk from an animal's udder
stethoscope   (n) a doctor's tool for listening to sounds inside the body
to suckle   (v) to give milk to from the breast or udder
veterinarian   (n) an animal doctor
to weed   (v) to take useless plants out of the ground

Now complete these sentences with words from Lists B and C. Change the form of a word if necessary.

1. A _____ can listen to an animal's heart with a _____ .

2. The sheep were in the _____ eating grass.

3. Many farmers use a _____ to move hay bales into their _____ .

Understanding the Picture

1. Which of these things do you see on this farm?

   a. an orchard   e. a pasture
   b. a toolbox   f. a chicken coop
   c. a field   g. a mailbox
   d. a plow   h. corn

2. Some of the people on this farm are having problems. Find someone who is having a problem with each of these things.

   a. a bull   c. eggs
   b. a hay bale   d. a goose

3. Which of these animals do you see on this farm?

a. goose
b. turkey
c. piglet (baby pig)
d. calf (baby cow)
e. bull

f. lamb (baby sheep)
g. goat
h. hen (female chicken)
i. cat
j. rabbit

What other animals do you see on this farm?

4. Which of these jobs are the people on this farm doing?

a. repairing a tractor
b. milking a cow
c. feeding a calf

d. unloading a truck
e. picking apples
f. weeding the garden

What other jobs are the people on this farm doing?

What Do You See?

Study this part of the picture. Then answer the questions.

1. What is the hen doing on the roof of the chicken coop?

2. What is happening in the garden?

3. What are the two men by the pickup truck doing?

4. What is happening in the hayloft?

5. What is the scarecrow's job? Is it doing its job?

What Are They Saying?

The man holding the tomato is talking to the woman in the yellow hat. Practice their conversation with a partner.

MAN: Did you see this tomato, Maggie?

WOMAN: Yes, I did. Isn't it big?

MAN: It's huge! What are you going to do with it?

WOMAN: I think I'll cut it up for our salad tonight.

MAN: That sounds good. You have a lot of nice-looking tomatoes this year.

WOMAN: Thank you. I'm going to take some over to Mrs. Malone this afternoon.

MAN: That's a good idea. I'm sure she'll enjoy them. Do you mind if I have one?

WOMAN: Didn't you eat breakfast?

MAN: Of course I did, but that was two hours ago—and I love tomatoes!

Now work with your partner to change the conversation so that

- The woman is going to use the big tomato to make spaghetti sauce.
- The woman is going to take some tomatoes to the farmer's market tomorrow.
- The man thinks she will sell a lot of tomatoes.
- The man ate a small breakfast.

Practice your new conversation together.

What Will Happen Next?

Answer these questions in small groups. Then compare your answers with those of the other groups.

1. What will happen to the man in the hayloft?

2. What will the man holding the tomato do next?

3. What will the two men by the pickup truck do next?

What Would You Say?

Act out this situation with a partner. Take turns playing parts A and B.

A. You are working in your garden. A friend comes to visit you. You offer to give your friend some green beans and strawberries. You are going to freeze some of your beans and strawberries.

B. You are visiting a friend who is working in his or her garden. You tell your friend how good the green beans and strawberries look. You ask what your friend will do with so many beans and strawberries.

What Do You See?

Study this part of the picture. Then answer the questions.

1. What are the veterinarians doing?

2. What is the girl in the pink pants doing?

3. What is happening in the barn?

4. What is the woman in the blue jeans doing?

5. What is the goose doing?

What Are They Saying?

The girl in the pink shorts (Betsy) is talking to the girl in the pink pants (Jill). Practice their conversation with a partner.

BETSY: Jill, can you help me?

JILL: What do you need?

BETSY: I'm dropping the eggs!

JILL: Oh, dear. Well, just a minute. The calf is almost finished with this bottle.

BETSY: All the eggs are breaking!

JILL: Put the basket down on the ground. I'll carry it to the house for you.

BETSY: There are more eggs to gather, but my basket is full.

JILL: *Too* full, it looks like. What a mess!

BETSY: I didn't mean to break the eggs.

JILL: I know. Here, I'll clean this up. Why don't you get another basket and gather the rest of the eggs?

Now work with your partner to change the conversation so that

- Betsy yells for someone to help her.
- Jill asks her what is wrong.
- Jill asks Steve (the boy in the blue shorts) to help Betsy.
- Betsy says Steve can't help her. He's running away from the goose.
- Jill tells Betsy to get a broom and clean up the mess.

Practice your new conversation together.

What Will Happen Next?

Answer these questions in small groups. Then compare your answers with those of the other groups.

1. What will happen to the boy in the blue shorts?

2. What will the girl in the pink shorts do next?

3. What will the veterinarians do next?

What Would You Say?

Act out this situation in groups of three. Take turns playing parts A, B, and C.

A. You are carrying two big bags of groceries into your house. You need help opening the door. You ring the doorbell and yell for someone to help you.

B. You are on a ladder painting inside the house. You don't want to get down and open the door.

C. You are changing the baby's diaper inside the house. You can't open the door right now.

Let's Practice

Farm families have many chores (jobs) to do. Some families use a job chart to show who must do certain chores every day or every week. Look at this job chart for the Wang family.

JOB CHART: August 12-18

Family members: Mom, Dad, Lian, Hoy, Chen

JOBS	M	T	W	Th	F	Sa	Su
Set the Table	Lian	Hoy	Chen	Lian	Hoy	Chen	Mom
Wash dishes	Hoy	Chen	Lian	Hoy	Chen	Lian	Dad
Vacuum the house		Lian					
Dust the house			Hoy				
Feed the cats	Chen	Chen	Chen	Chen	Chen	Chen	Chen
Feed the dog	Lian	Lian	Lian	Lian	Lian	Lian	Lian
Weed the garden	Mom			Dad			
Feed the chickens	Hoy	Hoy	Hoy	Hoy	Hoy	Hoy	Hoy
Gather eggs	Hoy	Hoy	Hoy	Hoy	Hoy	Hoy	Hoy
Feed the horses	Chen	Dad	Mom	Chen	Lian	Hoy	Dad
Feed the cows	Dad	Hoy	Mom	Lian	Mom	Lian	Dad
Milk the cows	Dad	Hoy	Mom	Lian	Mom	Lian	Dad

Now work with a partner to answer these questions about the Wang family's job chart.

A. 1. How many different jobs are on this job chart?
    2. How many days are on this job chart?
    3. How many people are in the Wang family?

B. 1. How many chores must the Wangs do every day?
    2. How many chores must the Wangs do once a week?
    3. How many chores must the Wangs do twice a week?
    4. How often must the Wangs gather eggs?
    5. How often must the Wangs weed the garden?
    6. How often must the Wangs vacuum the house?

C. 1. Which chores must Lian do on Tuesday?
    2. Which chores must Hoy do on Monday?
    3. Which chores must Chen do on Friday?
    4. Which chores must Mom do on Wednesday?
    5. Which chores must Dad do on Sunday?

D. 1. How many days must Chen feed the horses?
    2. How many days must Lian feed the dog?
    3. How many days must Hoy gather the eggs?
    4. How many days must Dad wash the dishes?
    5. How many days must Mom milk the cows?

Now work as a class to make a job chart for your classroom.

Let's Learn More

Read these paragraphs about farms in the United States.

Farming is a big business in the United States. However, only about five percent of Americans live on farms. With the help of modern farming **methods** and machines, this small number of farmers can produce enough food to feed the whole country—and much of the world.

Until the early 1900s, most Americans lived on farms. Their farms provided food, clothing, and other basic needs for their families. Today, most U.S. farmers do not try to produce everything they need. Instead, they grow just one or two kinds of **crops** or raise one kind of livestock. They sell their crops or animals each year to earn money.

Another change in farming is the modern use of fertilizers, **herbicides,** and **insecticides.** These substances can increase and improve farm products, but many Americans believe they are dangerous to people and to the **environment.**

In many ways, living on a farm in the United States is like living in a town. Most farmhouses are full of modern **appliances.** Farm children go to school in nearby cities or towns. However, farm life is different in some ways. Farmers often live far away from their neighbors and from shopping malls, supermarkets, and fast-food restaurants. Yet farm families can enjoy and learn about nature in ways that most Americans cannot.

Vocabulary Check

Study these words and their meanings.

appliance   (n) a household machine (such as a stove, washing machine, or refrigerator) that uses electricity or gas

crop   (n) grain, fruit, or vegetables grown by a farmer

environment   (n) the natural world, including the air, land, and water

herbicide   (n) a substance that kills certain kinds of plants

insecticide   (n) a substance that kills insects

method   (n) a way of doing something

Now find the words in the reading that have these meanings.

1. not the same

2. ways to do something

3. substances that kill plants

4. things a farmer grows

5. things that help plants grow

6. new; not from the past

7. make or create

8. farm animals

9. not safe

10. things to wear

Comprehension Check

Decide whether each sentence is true or false. If a sentence is false, change it to make it true.

1. Most U.S. farmers grow one or two kinds of crops or raise one kind of livestock.

2. About one-half of all Americans live on farms.

3. Farming provides a chance to see and learn about nature.

4. Today, most U.S. farmers produce everything their families need.

5. Americans agree that fertilizers, herbicides, and insecticides are safe for farmers to use.

Extension Activity

Make a list of farm animals on the board. Next to each animal, write the English word for the sound it makes (for example: horse—neigh). You may be able to think of more than one word for some animals (for example: dog—bow-wow, woof). Practice these sounds by learning and singing the song "Old MacDonald Had a Farm."

Next, make a list of the words for the animal sounds in your native language. When everyone is finished, have volunteers put their lists on the board and say the sounds for the class. The whole class should practice each sound.

Compare the sounds each animal makes. Talk about why animals "talk" differently in each language. Do animals really make different sounds in different parts of the world?

Chapter 4
A Thanksgiving Day Dinner

Warm-Up

❑ What is your favorite holiday? How does your family celebrate this holiday?

❑ Thanksgiving means just what its name says: a time for giving thanks. What are you thankful for?

Words to Know

A. Here are the names of some things you can find in a kitchen or dining room. Look for them in the picture.

apron	gravy boat	platter
bowl	napkin	pot
candle	pan	salt shaker
carving knife	pepper mill	silverware
dish towel	pitcher	tablecloth
glass	plate	wooden spoon

B. Here are some words you can use to talk about Thanksgiving. Look for examples of these objects and people in the picture.

cornucopia (n) a curved horn filled with fruits, vegetables, and grains as a symbol of plenty of food; a common Thanksgiving decoration

Indian corn (n) ears of corn with kernels of many colors; a common Thanksgiving decoration

Indians (n) American Indians, also called Native Americans; the first people to live in America

parade (n) a line of decorated vehicles and people moving through the streets of a city or town

Pilgrims (n) a group of people who came to America from England and settled at Plymouth in 1620

C. Study these words and their meanings. Then look for examples of these objects and activities in the picture.

to carve (v) to cut into slices

dessert (n) a sweet food to eat after a meal

front yard (n) the land between the front of a building and the street

guest (n) someone who is visiting

to lick (v) to touch with one's tongue

relatives (n) members of the same family

to scold (v) to speak angrily to a person who did something wrong

smoke (n) a cloud of tiny particles caused by something burning

to spill (v) to accidentally let something fall out of its container

to stir (v) to mix with a spoon

Now complete these sentences with words from Lists B and C. Change the form of a word if necessary.

1. I have a big family. I like to see my _____.

2. Charles made cherry pie for our _____ tonight.

3. Tina is playing outside in the _____ .

4. The _____ and the _____ ate the first Thanksgiving dinner in America.

Understanding the Picture

1. Which of these foods do you see in the picture?

   a. rolls   e. pizza
   b. hamburgers   f. sweet potatoes
   c. lettuce salad g. turkey
   d. cranberry sauce h. pineapple

2. What Thanksgiving decorations do you see in this house?

   a. a plant   e. a Pilgrim poster
   b. a turkey   f. a china cabinet
   c. a rug   g. a pumpkin
   d. a cornucopia h. Indian corn

3. Which of these objects are on the dining room table?

a. salt shaker
b. silverware
c. chair
d. candle
e. dish towel
f. tablecloth
g. turkey
h. mixing bowl
i. apron
j. gravy boat

4. Find someone in the picture who is doing each of these things.

a. bringing chairs to the table
b. watching a parade
c. putting food on the table
d. talking on the telephone
e. stirring food
f. greeting a guest
g. sleeping
h. spilling food

What Do You See?

Study this part of the picture. Then answer the questions.

1. Which room is this? What is it used for?

2. What is the white-haired woman doing?

3. What is the man with the beard doing?

4. What happened to the woman in the green blouse?

5. Why are so many things going wrong here?

What Are They Saying?

The girl in the pink sweat suit is talking to her boyfriend on the telephone. Practice their conversation with a partner.

GIRL: Robert! You're late! I asked you to come at 11:00.

BOY: I know. That's why I'm calling.

GIRL: What's wrong?

BOY: I'm sorry, Jennifer. I can't come over today. I have a terrible sore throat.

GIRL: Oh, no! Your voice does sound funny. When did you get sick?

BOY: Just this morning. I have a fever and a runny nose, too.

GIRL: I'm sorry you're not feeling well. I wanted you to meet my relatives.

BOY: I can't meet them like this!

GIRL: I guess you're right. Well, I'll call you tonight to see how you're feeling.

BOY: Okay. Happy Thanksgiving, Jennifer!

GIRL: Happy Thanksgiving to you too, Robert. I hope you feel better soon.

Now work with your partner to change the conversation so that

- Robert has a headache instead of a sore throat.
- Robert got sick last night.
- Jennifer wanted Robert to meet her grandparents.
- Jennifer asks Robert to call her tomorrow.

Practice your new conversation together.

What Will Happen Next?

Answer these questions in small groups. Then compare your answers with those of the other groups.

1. What will the boy in the blue-green sweater do next?

2. What will the man with the beard do next?

3. What will the two women by the door do next?

What Would You Say?

Act out this situation with a partner. Take turns playing parts A and B.

A. You invited a friend to go out for pizza with you this evening. You are getting ready to go when your friend calls on the telephone.

B. Your friend invited you to go out for pizza tonight. You were planning to go, but your mother has to work late today. She asked you to stay home and take care of your younger brothers. You are calling your friend to explain why you can't go out for pizza.

What Do You See?

Study this part of the picture. Then answer the questions.

1. Which room is this? What is it used for?

2. What are the man and boy by the Pilgrim poster doing?

3. What is the white-haired man doing with the knife?

4. What is the woman in the blue blouse doing?

5. What are the children at the small table doing?

What Are They Saying?

The woman in the long striped skirt wants to help with the meal. She stops talking to the man in the blue jacket and speaks to the woman in the pink dress. Practice their conversation with a partner.

WOMAN 1:   Excuse me, Amanda. Can I do anything to help?

WOMAN 2:   Oh, you're a guest today, Lois. Just enjoy yourself.

WOMAN 1:   I can't enjoy myself while all of you are working so hard. Please give me something to do.

WOMAN 2:   Well, okay. There's plenty of work! Will you please tell everyone in the living room that dinner will be ready in five minutes?

WOMAN 1:   Certainly.

WOMAN 2:   If you see Mom, will you ask her if she has any more chairs upstairs?

WOMAN 1:   Of course. I'll be back in a minute.

WOMAN 2:   Thanks a lot, Lois. I'm glad Richard invited you to come today.

WOMAN 1:   Thank you, Amanda. I'm very happy to be here.

Now work with your partner to change the conversation so that

- Amanda asks Lois to get some water glasses from the kitchen.
- Amanda asks Lois to find Mark and tell him to put the dog in the back yard.
- Lois says she will put the dog in the back yard herself. Then she will get the glasses.
- Amanda is glad that Lois and her husband are here today.

Practice your new conversation together.

What Will Happen Next?

Answer these questions in small groups. Then compare your answers with those of the other groups.

1. What will the boy in the short-sleeved red shirt do next?

2. What will happen to the dog?

3. What will the woman in the blue blouse do next?

What Would You Say?

Act out this situation in groups of three. Take turns playing parts A, B, and C.

A. You are spending the evening at a friend's house. You always help cook dinner at home, so you offer to help your friend's parents with the meal.

B. You invited a friend to spend the evening at your house. You want your friend to watch TV with you while your parents cook dinner.

C. You are B's father. You are surprised when A offers to help cook dinner.

Let's Practice

Here is a recipe for pumpkin pie. Read the recipe.
Then work in groups to answer the questions.

From the Kitchen of Aunt Betty
Pumpkin Pie

Ingredients
1 pie crust
2 eggs, slightly beaten
2 cups canned pumpkin
¾ cup sugar
½ tsp. salt

1 tsp. ground cinnamon
½ tsp. ground ginger
¼ tsp. ground cloves
1⅓ cups evaporated milk

Directions: Heat oven to 425°F. Mix filling ingredients in bowl. Pour into prepared pie crust. Bake at 425° for 15 minutes. Reduce heat to 350° and continue baking 35 to 40 minutes, or until knife inserted in center comes out clean. Cool completely before serving.

Understanding the Recipe

This recipe uses two standard American units of measure: the **teaspoon** (tsp.) and the **cup.** One teaspoon equals 5 milliliters. One cup equals 240 milliliters.

To measure the ingredients for this pie, you will need a measuring cup and a set of measuring spoons.

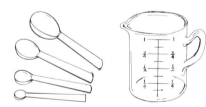

Preparing to Bake

1. How many ingredients do you need to make this pie?

2. You have sugar, eggs, and salt at home. What ingredients do you need to buy at the supermarket?

3. You need a measuring cup and a set of measuring spoons to make this pumpkin pie. What other equipment do you need?

Following the Recipe

1. How hot should the oven be when you put in the pie?

2. How long should you bake the pie?

3. How can you tell if the pie is done?

Changing the Recipe

This recipe makes one pumpkin pie. If you want to make two pies, how much of each ingredient will you need?

1. eggs

2. canned pumpkin

3. sugar

4. salt

5. ground cloves

Let's Learn More

Read these paragraphs about Thanksgiving.

Thanksgiving is a national holiday in the United States. It is celebrated each year on the fourth Thursday of November. On this day, families and friends traditionally **share** a special meal of turkey and other foods such as **stuffing,** sweet potatoes, cranberry sauce, and pumpkin pie.

Americans first celebrated Thanksgiving in Plymouth Colony in the early 1620s. The people living in this **colony** were called Pilgrims. They came to America to find religious freedom. Their first winter in America was a hard one, and many of the Pilgrims died. After their first good **harvest,** they chose a day to thank God for helping them through their difficult time. The Pilgrims invited their friends, the Native American Indians, to share in a big meal. Wild turkey, Indian corn, and pumpkins were probably some of the foods they ate. Today, the two main parts of an American Thanksgiving celebration are the same as they were more than 350 years ago: eating a big dinner and thanking God for the good things in one's life.

Another Thanksgiving tradition is watching parades. Many cities and towns have parades on Thanksgiving Day. Thousands of people stand in the streets to watch the parades. Others watch them at home on TV. Because Thanksgiving "officially" starts the Christmas **season,** Santa Claus appears at the end of every Thanksgiving parade.

Vocabulary Check

Study these words and their meanings.

colony   (n) an area of land that is ruled by
   another country
harvest   (n) the gathering of grains, fruits, and
   vegetables when they are ready to eat
season   (n) a certain time of the year
to share   (v) to have or use with other people
stuffing   (n) a mixture of foods such as bread, celery,
   and onion that is cooked inside a chicken or turkey

Now look at the words in these lists. Find a word in List B that goes with each word in List A.

A	B
1. religious freedom	turkey
2. stuffing	food
3. parade	America
4. harvest	Indians
5. Pilgrims	Santa Claus

Comprehension Check

Choose the best answer for each question.

1. What are the two main parts of an American Thanksgiving celebration?

   a. harvesting food and eating a big dinner
   b. watching parades and giving thanks to God
   c. eating a big dinner and giving thanks to God

2. When is Thanksgiving celebrated?

   a. the fourth Tuesday of November
   b. the fourth Thursday of November
   c. the first Thursday of November

3. Who lived in Plymouth Colony?

   a. the Pilgrims   c. the Indians
   b. Santa Claus

4. What foods do Americans traditionally eat on Thanksgiving Day?

   a. pumpkin pie and applesauce
   b. turkey and stuffing
   c. all of the above

5. Why did the Pilgrims come to America?

   a. to find the Indians   c. to find religious
   b. to find food   freedom

Extension Activity

Thanksgiving is a time for people to enjoy their families and friends, good food, and all the other good things in their lives. However, many people in the United States (and in other countries) don't have good food to eat or homes and families to enjoy.

In groups of three, talk about some ways the students at your school could help hungry and/or homeless people in your city or town. Make a list of your ideas. Then choose the best idea from your list. Tell the rest of the class about your idea.

As a class, talk about all the ideas. Which ones are the best for your school? Vote on the three best ideas. Then write a class letter to your school principal. Tell about your three ideas. Ask if the school can try one of your ideas to help hungry and/or homeless people. Invite the principal to visit your class to give his or her answer.

Unit Two

Around Town

In cities and towns all over the United States, Americans participate in daily activities such as shopping, mailing letters, and dealing with money. In this unit, you will learn and practice the language Americans use every day in a variety of common situations.

Chapter 5: At the Bank takes us to a large city bank. You will study and talk about many of the services provided by American banks, such as checking accounts, safe-deposit boxes, automatic teller machines, and drive-up tellers.

Chapter 6: At the Post Office shows how the U.S. Postal Service works. You will practice buying stamps and mailing letters, and you will talk about the other services available at an American post office.

Chapter 7: At the Supermarket and **Chapter 8: At a Fast-Food Restaurant** focus on the important topic of buying food. You will learn how to shop in a typical American supermarket and practice ordering a meal in a fast-food restaurant.

Chapter 9: Emergency Services ends the unit with a look at some services that are available to help people in the United States. You will learn what to do in an emergency situation and how to get help from police officers, fire fighters, and paramedics. You will also talk about ways to prevent fires and prepare yourselves for other emergencies.

Chapter 5
At the Bank

Warm-Up

❑ Why do people go to a bank?   ❑ When do you go to the bank?

Words to Know

A. Here are the names of some things you can find at a bank. Look for them in the picture.

automatic teller   computer   safe-deposit
  machine (ATM)   counter   box
bill   drive-up teller   teller
coin   guard   vault
                                         window

B. Here are some other words you can use to talk about banking. Study these words and their meanings.

balance (n) the amount of money in a bank account

to borrow (v) to take something you plan to return

to cash a check (v) to get money for a check

check (n) a paper that tells a bank to pay a certain amount of money to a certain person

checking account (n) an agreement with a bank that lets a customer write checks to pay for things

to deposit (v) to put (money) into a bank account

foreign currency exchange (n) a place to trade money of one country for money of another country

interest (n) (1) money that a bank pays people who have money in a bank account (2) money that a bank charges people who borrow money from the bank

loan (n) money borrowed from a bank for a certain amount of time

to open/close an account (v) to start/end an agreement with a bank that lets you use the bank's services

receipt (n) a paper that tells how much money a person put in or took out of a bank account

to rent (v) to pay money to use something for a certain amount of time

savings account (n) an agreement with a bank that lets a customer save money safely and earn interest

to withdraw (v) to take out of a bank account

C. Here are more words you can use to talk about the objects and activities in the picture.

escalator   to roller-skate   stroller
piggy bank   roller skates   to wait in line
rattle   skateboard   yo-yo

Now complete these sentences with words from Lists A and B. Change the form of a word if necessary.

1. Maggie wrote a _____ to pay for her groceries.

2. Dan got a _____ from the bank to buy a new car.

3. Sam keeps his important papers in a _____ .

4. Josie _____ a check to get money for our lunch.

5. I _____ ten dollars from my bank account.

Understanding the Picture

1. Which of these things can you do at this bank?

    a. rent a safe-deposit box
    b. buy currency of another country
    c. ask for a loan
    d. buy a bus ticket
    e. go to a drive-up teller
    f. withdraw money at an automatic teller machine

2. Many people are working at this bank. Which of these jobs are they doing?

    a. using the automatic teller machine
    b. guarding the vault
    c. giving directions
    d. writing a check
    e. using a computer
    f. talking on the telephone

3. Find the place(s) in the picture where you can do each of these things.

   a. borrow money
   b. get cash from a machine
   c. withdraw money from your savings account
   d. deposit money without leaving your car
   e. keep important papers and valuable things
   f. cash a check

4. There are many customers at this bank. Which of these things are they doing?

   a. taking things out of a safe-deposit box
   b. buying pennies
   c. waiting in line
   d. asking for a loan
   e. depositing money
   f. talking on the telephone

Study this part of the picture. Then answer the questions.

1. What is the child giving the teller?

2. Why is the child in the stroller crying?

3. What is the white-haired man doing?

4. What is the woman in the purple suit doing?

5. What is the man with the gun doing?

What Are They Saying?

The white-haired man is talking to the bank teller. Practice their conversation with a partner.

TELLER: May I help you?

MAN: Yes. I want to deposit some money in my savings account.

TELLER: How much money?

MAN: Everything that's in this jar.

TELLER: Okay, I'll have it counted. Just a minute, please.

(pause)

TELLER: That was a lot of pennies! Your total is $28.74.

MAN: I saved my pennies in that jar for more than a year.

TELLER: Please write your name and account number on this deposit slip.

MAN: Here you are.

TELLER: Thank you. Here's your receipt.

MAN: Thanks. May I have my jar back, too?

TELLER: Oh, sorry, I forgot. Here it is.

MAN: Thank you very much. I want to use it to save more pennies!

Now work with your partner to change the conversation so that

- The man wants to deposit the money in his checking account.
- The man's total is $35.21.
- The man saved his pennies for two years.
- The teller remembers to give the man his jar.

Practice your new conversation together.

What Will Happen Next?

Answer these questions in small groups. Then compare your answers with those of the other groups.

1. What will the man with the gun do next?

2. What will the boy with the skateboard do when he leaves the bank?

3. What will happen to the child in the stroller?

What Would You Say?

Act out this situation with a partner. Take turns playing parts A and B.

A. You are at the bank. You tell a bank teller that you want to withdraw fifty dollars from your savings account.

B. You are a bank teller. A customer wants to withdraw some money. You ask the customer to fill out a withdrawal slip. Then you give the customer the money and a receipt.

What Do You See?

Study this part of the picture. Then answer the questions.

1. What is the white-haired woman doing?

2. What is happening on the escalator?

3. What is the woman with the red glasses doing?

4. Where is the foreign currency exchange?

5. What is the bank guard doing?

What Are They Saying?

The bank guard is giving directions to the woman in the orange dress. Practice their conversation with a partner.

WOMAN: Excuse me. Where should I go to ask for a loan?

GUARD: Mr. Jackson in the loan department can help you. He's at the second desk on your right.

WOMAN: I need to rent a safe-deposit box, too.

GUARD: The vault is behind me, next to the bank director's office.

WOMAN: How late is the bank open today?

GUARD: We're open until 5:00.

WOMAN: Thanks very much for your help.

GUARD: No problem. Have a nice day.

Now work with your partner to change the conversation so that

- The woman needs to do these two things at the bank: (1) open a savings account and (2) exchange some American dollars for Brazilian cruzados.
- The woman asks if the bank is open on Saturdays.

Practice your new conversation together.

What Will Happen Next?

Answer these questions in small groups. Then compare your answers with those of the other groups.

1. What will happen to the boy on the escalator?

2. What will the white-haired woman do next?

3. What will the woman in the blue blouse do next?

What Would You Say?

Act out this situation with a partner. Take turns playing parts A and B.

A. You are new in town. You walk into the bank and see a guard near the door. You ask the guard where you should go to open a checking account and rent a safe-deposit box.

B. You are a bank guard. You know that a personal banker can help a customer open a checking account. The personal banking department is to the right, just past the loan department. You know that the guard at the vault can help a customer rent a safe-deposit box.

Let's Practice

Felipe Martinez has a checking account at the Big Savers Bank. In his **checkbook register,** he writes information about the checks he writes and about his deposits and withdrawals. Look at this page from Felipe's checkbook register.

NUMBER	DATE	TRANSACTION	PAYMENT	DEPOSIT	BALANCE
					234 92
—	6/1	deposit paycheck		655.00	+655.00
					889.92
216	6/3	Illinois Bell Telephone	18.80		-18.80
					871.12
217	6/7	Dr. Stuart (check-up)	60.00		-60.00
					811.12
—	6/11	ATM Withdrawal	30.00		-30.00
					781.12
218	6/12	Visa bill (full payment)	421.96		-421.96
					359.16
—	6/18	deposit paycheck		655.00	+655.00
					1014.16
219	6/21	Steve (baseball tickets)	22.00		-22.00
					992.16
220	6/25	D&D Housing (July rent)	802.75		-802.75
					189.41
221	6/30	Dino Oil Co. (gas)	17.43		-17.43
					171.98

FELIPE R. MARTINEZ
1247 GALENA RD.
EVANSTON, IL 60201

222

July 1, 19 93

PAY TO THE ORDER OF _Illinois Power Co._ $ 31.45

Thirty-One and 45/100 DOLLARS

BIG $AVER$ BANK
EVANSTON, IL

MEMO _____ _Felipe R. Martinez_

0579826   00219   222

FELIPE R. MARTINEZ
1247 GALENA RD.
EVANSTON, IL 60201

223

July 11, 19 93

PAY TO THE ORDER OF _Drake's Furniture_ $ 297.83

Two Hundred Ninety-Seven and 83/100 DOLLARS

BIG $AVER$ BANK
EVANSTON, IL

MEMO _Sofa_ _Felipe R. Martinez_

0579826   00219   223

Now work with a partner to answer these questions.

Understanding the Checkbook Register

1. How many checks did Felipe write in June?

2. How much money did Felipe deposit in June?

3. What was the amount of Felipe's biggest check?

4. What was Felipe's lowest balance in June?

5. What was Felipe's highest balance in June?

6. What did Felipe do on June 11?

BIG $AVER$ BANK
EVANSTON, IL

Thank you for your deposit. This is your transaction receipt.

Account: 0579826 00219
Date: 7-10-93
Deposit: $655.00

BIG $AVER$ MONEY MACHINE

✱ ✱ ✱ ✱ ✱ ✱

DATE   TIME
07/05/93 10:49

MACHINE NO.
IL 55432

CARD NO.
6914566-2809

WITHDRAWAL $50.00

FROM CHECKING
057982600219

THANK YOU!

Using a Checkbook Register

Make a new page for Felipe's checkbook register on a piece of paper. Include all six columns you see above. Now look at these checks, bank receipt, and ATM receipt. Write about them on the page you made for Felipe's checkbook register. Add and subtract the amounts carefully in the balance column.

Making a Checkbook Register

Make another checkbook register on a piece of paper. Then make up five "checks" and two "receipts" and give them to your partner. Let your partner write the information about them in his or her checkbook register. Write the information about your partner's checks and receipts in your checkbook register. Then look at each other's work. Did your partner add or subtract each amount correctly in the balance column?

Let's Learn More

Read these paragraphs about banks in the United States.

The United States has more than fifty thousand banks. Many Americans borrow money from banks to pay for their houses, cars, and other big **expenses.** Banks also provide a safe place for people to keep their money. The federal government **insures** most bank deposits so customers will not lose their money if a bank becomes **bankrupt.**

Savings accounts and checking accounts are available at most banks. Many U.S. banks also offer safe-deposit boxes, foreign currency exchanges, **traveler's checks,** and help with loans and **investments.** Some banks offer credit cards. These small plastic cards provide an easy way for people to pay for things. Nearly half of Americans have credit cards.

Many Americans use automatic teller machines (ATMs) to deposit and withdraw money and to **transfer** money from one bank account to another. ATMs are popular because people can use them twenty-four hours a day, seven days a week. Most U.S. cities and towns have ATMs in convenient places such as shopping centers and gas stations. Drive-up tellers are another popular service offered by some American banks. Customers who use the drive-up tellers can withdraw or deposit money without leaving their cars. Most U.S. banks work hard to **attract** new customers and to keep their old customers happy.

Vocabulary Check

Study these words and their meanings.

to attract   (v) to make someone want to come nearer
bankrupt   (adj) ruined financially
expense   (n) something that costs money
to insure   (v) to protect against loss
investment   (n) a purchase used to make more money
to transfer   (v) to move from one place to another
traveler's check   (n) a check you can buy at a bank to use when traveling

Now choose the best word to complete each sentence.

1. The Holts had two big _____ this month. They bought a new car and had a baby. (expenses, credit cards)

2. Our bank is adding a drive-up teller to try to _____ more customers. (attract, borrow)

3. Stan's _____ in that computer company made him rich. (traveler's check, investment)

4. If the federal government _____ deposits in your bank, the money in your accounts will be safe. (transfers, insures)

5. Many people need a _____ from a bank when they buy a new car or a house. (loan, deposit)

Comprehension Check

Match each bank service with its purpose.

1. credit cards
2. safe-deposit boxes
3. automatic teller machines
4. savings accounts
5. checking accounts
6. drive-up tellers
7. loans

a. allow customers to save money safely

b. allow customers to borrow money to pay for big expenses

c. allow customers to deposit or withdraw money without getting out of their cars

d. allow customers to write checks to pay for things

e. allow customers to deposit or withdraw money 24 hours a day, seven days a week

f. provide a safe place to keep valuable things

g. allow customers to pay for things without using cash or a check

Extension Activity

In "families" of three or four, make a **budget** (a plan for spending money) for one month. Your family's **income** (money coming in) is $800 a month.

First make a list of the things you will need to pay for (food, clothes, telephone, electricity, rent, and so forth). Then decide how much money you can spend on each thing.

If you have any extra money, talk about what to do with it. Will you put it in a savings account? Why or why not?

Present your budget to the class and listen to the other groups tell about their budgets. In what ways are they the same as yours? In what ways are they different? Which budget does the class think is the best? Why?

Chapter 6
At the Post Office

Warm-Up

❏ Why do people go to a post office?

❏ How often do you go to the post office? What do you do at the post office?

Words to Know

A. Here are the names of some things you can find at a post office. Look for them in the picture.

American flag	mail carrier	post office box
change machine	mail slot	scale
counter	package	stamp
envelope	postal worker	stamp machine
letter	postmaster	window

B. Here are some other words you can use to talk about mail service. Study these words and their meanings.

address (n) a person's building number, street name, city, state, and ZIP code

airmail (n) mail that travels by airplane

to deliver mail (v) to take mail to an address

express mail (n) the fastest U.S. mail service. Express mail is delivered the day after it is sent.

first-class mail (n) the standard mail service used for letters, postcards, and small packages

to insure an item (v) to arrange to get money if something is lost or broken in the mail

metered mail (n) mail that has a mark from a machine called a postage meter instead of a stamp

money order (n) a special check you can buy at a post office and safely send through the mail

parcel post (n) a type of mail service for packages that weigh more than one pound

passport (n) a government paper that allows a person to travel to other countries

postage (n) the cost of mailing something; stamps

registered mail (n) mail that is insured

to sort (v) to put things into groups

ZIP code (n) the number of a postal delivery area in the United States

C. Here are some words you can use to talk about the objects and activities in the picture.

to lick	to wait in line
to swing	to weigh
twine	to wrap a package

Now complete these sentences with words from List B. Change the form of a word if necessary.

1. If you are sending a letter that must arrive the next day, send it by _____.

2. If you are sending a big package that doesn't need to arrive quickly, send it by _____.

3. Use _____ to send a letter or a postcard.

4. If you are sending a letter to another country and you want it to arrive in a few days, send it by _____.

5. Never send cash in the mail. Send a _____ instead.

Understanding the Picture

1. There are many customers at this post office. Which of these things are they doing?

   a. delivering mail
   b. writing letters
   c. mailing letters
   d. buying packages
   e. waiting in line
   f. applying for passports
   g. buying stamps
   h. looking for ZIP codes

2. Find the place(s) in the picture where you can do each of these things.

   a. buy stamps
   b. mail a package
   c. receive mail
   d. apply for a passport
   e. get change for a dollar
   f. buy a money order
   g. mail a letter
   h. weigh a package

3. There are many employees at this post office. Which of these jobs are they doing?

a. going out to deliver mail
b. waiting in line
c. sorting mail
d. selling money orders
e. writing letters
f. helping customers
g. selling stamps
h. selling ZIP codes

4. Find someone in the picture who is doing each of these things.

a. putting stamps on an envelope
b. helping someone
c. asking a question
d. throwing something away
e. dropping something

What Do You See?

Study this part of the picture. Then answer the questions.

1. What is the problem at the parcel post window?

2. What is the man in the green shirt and blue jeans doing?

3. What are the postal workers doing behind the counter?

4. What is happening at the window by the scale?

5. What is the man in the tan jacket doing? Why?

What Are They Saying?

The man in the green shirt is talking to the postal worker at the "stamps only" window. Practice their conversation with a partner.

POSTAL WORKER: May I help you?

MAN: Yes. I need fifty stamps.

POSTAL WORKER: First-class stamps?

MAN: Yes. Do you have any with pretty pictures?

POSTAL WORKER: We have these birds and these flowers.

MAN: I'll take the birds, please.

POSTAL WORKER: Do you need anything else?

MAN: Yes. I need ten airmail stamps, too.

POSTAL WORKER: Okay. That comes to twenty dollars.

MAN: Will you take a check?

POSTAL WORKER: Yes, if you show me your driver's license.

MAN: Okay. Here you are.

POSTAL WORKER: Thank you. Have a nice day.

Now work with your partner to change the conversation so that

• The man needs one hundred stamps.
• The postal worker shows him three kinds of stamps.
• The man doesn't need anything else.
• The total is thirty dollars.
• The man gives the postal worker two twenty-dollar bills.

Practice your new conversation together.

What Will Happen Next?

Answer these questions in small groups. Then compare your answers with those of the other groups.

1. What will the customer at the parcel post window do next?

2. What will the postal worker by the scale do next?

3. What will the man in the tan jacket do next?

What Would You Say?

Act out this situation with a partner. Take turns playing parts A and B.

A. You are buying stamps at the post office. You ask if you can use your credit card to pay for them.

B. You are a postal worker at the "stamps only" window. You know that the post office doesn't take credit cards. Customers can pay with cash or checks.

What Do You See?

Study this part of the picture. Then answer the questions.

1. What is the man in the orange shirt doing?

2. What is the mail carrier by the door doing?

3. What is the woman in the purple shirt doing?

4. What is happening to the man with the cane?

5. Where can you mail a letter without going into the post office?

What Are They Saying?

The woman in the purple shirt is talking to the mail carrier. Practice their conversation with a partner.

WOMAN: Excuse me. I have a question.

MAIL CARRIER: Yes?

WOMAN: I want to send this letter airmail to Colombia. Which slot should I put it in?

MAIL CARRIER: You can put it in the "stamped mail" slot.

WOMAN: Thank you. Do postcards go in that slot, too?

MAIL CARRIER: Yes. You can put anything with a stamp on it in that slot, if it will fit!

WOMAN: I understand. Thanks for your help.

MAIL CARRIER: No problem. Have a nice day.

Now work with your partner to change the conversation so that

• The woman asks what "express mail" means.
• The mail carrier explains that express mail travels very quickly. It is delivered the day after it is mailed.
• The woman asks if she can put her letter in the express mail slot so it will arrive the next day.
• The mail carrier tells her she will have to pay about ten dollars to send her letter by express mail.
• The woman decides to put her letter in the "stamped mail" slot.

Practice your new conversation together.

What Will Happen Next?

Answer these questions in small groups. Then compare your answers with those of the other groups.

1. What will the man with the cane do next?

2. What will the two mail carriers do next?

3. What will the woman in the orange dress do inside the post office?

What Would You Say?

Act out this situation in groups of three. Take turns playing parts A, B, and C.

A. You are standing outside the post office with an important letter to mail. You want to know when it will go out if you put it in the "stamped mail" slot.

B. You are mailing letters from work. They have marks from the office postage meter. You don't know which slot to use.

C. You are a mail carrier. You see two people by the mail slots. You ask if they need help. You know that the mail goes out every hour. You look at B's letters and tell him to use the "metered mail" slot.

Let's Practice

In order to use the U.S. Postal Service, you must correctly prepare your letters or packages for mailing. All mail must have a stamp (or mark from a postage meter) and a delivery address. A return address is also helpful, in case your mail cannot be delivered to the delivery address.

Here is an envelope that is ready for mailing. Work with a partner to answer the questions about this envelope.

BRUCE CAMPOBELLO
976 W. FOURTEENTH ST.
SAN FRANCISCO, CA 94188

MS. MARTINE VILLANOVA
1216 FAIRBANKS DR.
NOVI, MI 48050

1. What is the **sender's** name? (Who is sending this letter?)

2. What is the **recipient's** name? (Who will receive this letter?)

3. What state does the sender live in?

4. What state does the recipient live in?

5. What is the sender's street address?

6. What is the recipient's ZIP code?

Now follow these directions to practice mailing your own letter:

1. Ask your partner for his or her mailing address. Be sure to get the building number, street name, city, state, and ZIP code. If you don't know how to spell your partner's name or any of the other words, ask!

2. Prepare an "envelope" to send to your partner. Use your own address for the return address. Use your partner's address for the delivery address. Remember to use the correct ZIP codes and the correct two-letter abbreviation for your state. Don't forget to draw a "stamp" in the corner, too!

3. "Mail" your letter in a box on your teacher's desk. The teacher will sort and deliver your mail. If you prepared your envelope correctly, the teacher will deliver it to your partner. If not, the teacher will return it to you—or keep it in a "dead letter" box!

Let's Learn More

Read these paragraphs about the U.S. postal system.

The United States Postal Service is the largest mail service in the world. Each year, it delivers more than 140 billion pieces of mail—almost half the mail that is sent worldwide. There are more than 40,000 post offices in the United States.

The American postal system began in the 1700s, and its services **improved** and **increased** in the 1800s. Postage stamps were first used in 1847, mailboxes in 1853, and registered mail in 1855. The post office has often been quick to use new types of transportation. Mail was first carried by railroad in 1862, and airmail service began in 1918.

The U.S. Postal Service is a government-owned corporation that offers a variety of services. People can buy stamps, send letters and packages, get information on postal **rates,** and buy postal money orders at any post office. Americans can also **apply for** passports and **rent** post office boxes at many post offices.

Several kinds of mail service are available in the United States. First-class mail is used for most letters, greeting cards, postcards, and other personal mail. Fourth-class mail (parcel post) can be used for packages weighing one pound or more. Express mail is the U.S. Postal Service's fastest service. Items that are sent by express mail are delivered the next day. The cost of mailing a letter or package depends on the weight of the item and the type of mail service used.

Vocabulary Check

Study these words and their meanings.

to apply for   (v) to officially ask for, usually in writing
to improve   (v) to get better
to increase   (v) to grow in number or size
rate   (n) price; cost
to rent   (v) to pay money to use something for a certain amount of time

Now find words in the reading that mean the opposite of these words and phrases.

1. slow
2. got worse
3. smallest
4. receive
5. decreased
6. sell
7. less
8. old
9. ended
10. seldom; rarely

Comprehension Check

Choose the best word or phrase to complete each sentence.

passports	money orders
postage stamps	airmail
corporation	parcel post

1. The U.S. Postal Service is a _____ that is owned by the federal government.

2. The U.S. postal system began to provide _____ service in 1918.

3. Packages that weigh more than one pound can be sent by _____.

4. Americans can apply for _____ at some post offices.

5. _____ were first used by the U.S. Postal Service in 1847.

Extension Activity

Imagine that you just moved to the United States. You want to send a letter to a friend in your native country, but you don't know how to mail a letter in the United States. A neighbor offers to help you. In groups of three, make a list of five questions you should ask your neighbor.

Exchange questions with another group and try to answer the other group's questions while they try to answer yours. Do the two groups agree on the answers to all ten questions? If not, write the "problem" questions on the blackboard.

With the whole class, talk about the questions on the board. Can you agree on answers to all the questions? If not, write a class letter to the postmaster at your local post office. Ask your "problem" questions. Mail your letter, and then wait for an answer to your questions!

Chapter 7
At the Supermarket

Warm-Up

❑ What can you buy at a supermarket?

❑ Where does your family usually shop for food? Why?

Words to Know

A. Here are the names of some things you can find at a supermarket. Look for them in the picture.

aisle	dairy case	meat counter
bagger	delicatessen (deli)	produce
canned goods	employee	scale
cash register	express lane	service desk
cashier	fish counter	shelves
checkout counter	frozen foods	shopping cart

B. Here are some other words you can use to talk about a supermarket. Study these words and their meanings.

brand   (n) a company's name for a product

butcher   (n) a person who cuts up and sells meat

carton   (n) a box made of hard paper

to check out   (v) to take items to a counter and pay for them

coupon   (n) a piece of paper that gives you a certain amount (such as fifty cents) off the price of an item

groceries   (n) food and household supplies

to ring up   (v) to use a cash register to add the prices of the items a customer is buying

sample   (n) a small piece of something

to weigh   (v) to use a scale to find out how heavy something is

C. Here are the names of some foods and other products you can buy at a supermarket. Look for them in the picture.

bread	ham	pork chop
celery	lettuce	salami
cheese	lobster	sausage
chicken	onion	squash
detergent	orange	steak
doughnut	paper towels	toilet paper
fish	pear	tomato
grapes	pie	watermelon

Now complete these sentences with words from Lists A and B. Change the form of a word if necessary.

1. Which _____ of orange juice do you want?
   I'll take Golden Sun. I have a _____ for twenty cents off that kind.

2. You can pay for your _____ at a checkout counter. If you are buying only a few items, you can use an _____ .

3. You can find lettuce in the _____ department.

Understanding the Picture

1. Which of these items do you see at this supermarket?

   a. toilet paper   f. ham
   b. bread   g. milk
   c. bananas   h. ice cream
   d. cherries   i. pie
   e. orange juice   j. lobster

2. There are many employees at this supermarket. Which of these jobs are they doing?

   a. bagging groceries
   b. helping people at the deli
   c. pushing carts
   d. mopping the floor
   e. ringing up customers' groceries

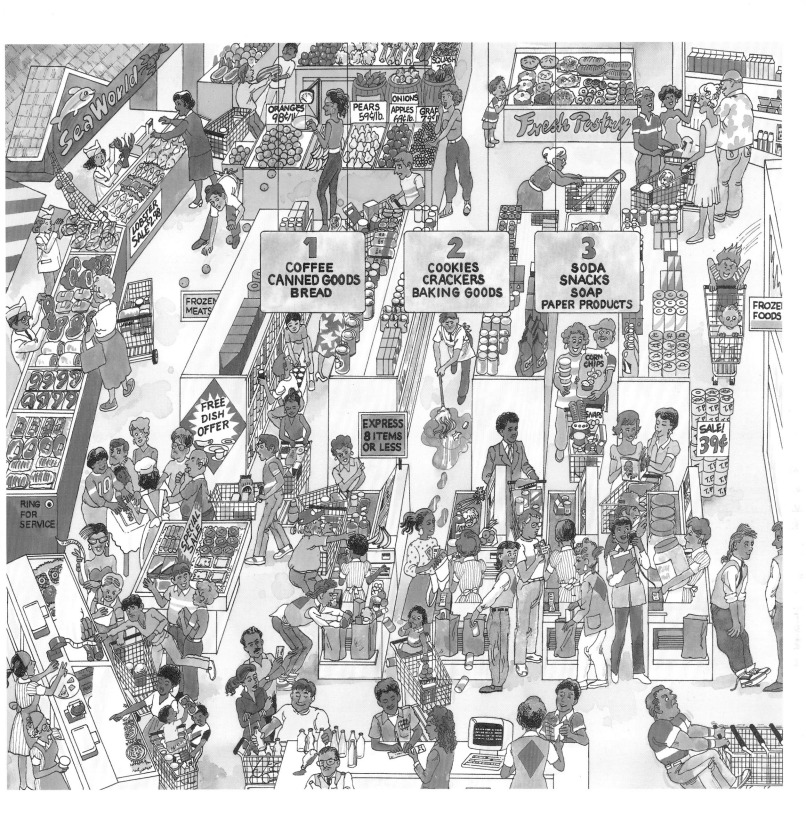

3. Some of the people at this supermarket are having problems. Which of these problems do you see?

  a. A man can't separate one cart from the others.
  b. A woman fell down in aisle 3.
  c. A lobster is pinching an employee's finger.
  d. A child can't reach the cookies.
  e. Two customers are fighting about a watermelon.

4. Which of these people are doing things they should **not** do at this supermarket?

  a. the two employees who are talking instead of working
  b. the man who is buying many items in the express lane
  c. the woman who is eating a grape
  d. the boy who is tasting a cake
  e. the two women who are looking at a magazine
  f. the boy who is running and pushing a cart

What Do You See?

Study this part of the picture. Then answer the questions.

1. Why is the woman in the blue shirt pointing to the sign?

2. What is the woman with the white hat doing?

3. What is the woman with the purple sunglasses doing?

4. What is happening to the customer's food in the express lane?

5. What is the white-haired man in the pink shirt doing?

What Are They Saying?

The woman in the white blouse is talking to one of the employees at the deli. Practice their conversation with a partner.

EMPLOYEE: Number 73!

CUSTOMER: That's me. I need a pound of sliced ham, please.

EMPLOYEE: Which brand do you want, Cole's or Gold Star?

CUSTOMER: How much are they?

EMPLOYEE: Cole's is $3.99 a pound, and Gold Star is $3.29 a pound.

CUSTOMER: I'll take Gold Star, please.

(pause)

EMPLOYEE: Here you go. Can I get you anything else?

CUSTOMER: Yes. I'll take half a pound of potato salad, too.

EMPLOYEE: It's on sale today for ninety-nine cents a pound.

CUSTOMER: Great! Is the macaroni salad on sale, too?

EMPLOYEE: No, it isn't.

CUSTOMER: Okay.

EMPLOYEE: Here's your potato salad. Will that be all?

CUSTOMER: Yes. Thank you very much.

Now work with your partner to change the conversation so that

- The customer wants turkey, not ham.
- The employee asks if she wants plain turkey or smoked turkey.
- The macaroni salad is on sale today.
- The customer wants half a pound of macaroni salad, too.

Practice your new conversation together.

What Will Happen Next?

Answer these questions in small groups. Then compare your answers with those of the other groups.

1. What will happen to the boy in the yellow shirt by the deli?

2. What will the man in the purple shirt and brown slacks do next?

3. What will the man in the brown sweater and blue pants by the deli do next?

What Would You Say?

Act out this situation with a partner. Take turns playing parts A and B.

A. It's your turn to order at the supermarket deli. You ask how much the turkey, roast beef, fruit salad, and potato salad cost. Then you order a pound of meat and a pound of salad.

B. You are an employee at the supermarket deli. You know the price of each item. The roast beef and the fruit salad are on sale today.

What Do You See?

Study this part of the picture. Then answer the questions.

1. What is happening in aisle 2?

2. What are the baggers doing?

3. What kinds of food are the couple in aisle 3 buying?

4. What is the little girl in the cart doing?

5. What are the cashiers doing?

What Are They Saying?

The woman in the yellow blouse is talking to the cashier. Practice their conversation with a partner.

CASHIER: Your total is $63.48.

CUSTOMER: I have these coupons, too.

CASHIER: Okay. *(pause)* That's $59.98.

CUSTOMER: Can I write my check for more than that?

CASHIER: If you have one of our check-cashing cards, you can write a check for up to thirty dollars more than your total.

CUSTOMER: Okay. Here you go.

CASHIER: May I see your check-cashing card, please?

CUSTOMER: Oh, sure. I'm sorry.

CASHIER: No problem. Here's your change and your receipt. Have a nice day.

Now work with your partner to change the conversation so that

- The cashier asks the customer if she has any coupons.
- The customer doesn't have any coupons.
- The customer doesn't have a check-cashing card.
- Only customers with check-cashing cards can write checks for more than their total.
- The cashier wants to see the customer's driver's license.

Practice your new conversation together.

What Will Happen Next?

Answer these questions in small groups. Then compare your answers with those of the other groups.

1. What will happen in the aisle by the frozen foods?

2. What will the couple in aisle 3 do next?

3. What will happen to the little girl in the cart?

What Would You Say?

Act out this situation with a partner. Take turns playing parts A and B.

A. You are a supermarket cashier. You just rang up a customer's groceries. The total is $37.61. You ask if the customer has any coupons. At your store, customers can pay with a check if they have a driver's license or a check-cashing card.

B. You are at the supermarket checkout counter. You don't have any coupons. You ask the cashier if you can write a check for your groceries.

Let's Practice

Look at this newspaper advertisement for PriceRight Supermarket.
The ad shows sale prices for some items. It has coupons for other items.

Work in small groups to answer these questions
about the advertisement.

Understanding the Ad

1. When will the items in this ad be on sale?

2. What is the sale price for a dozen eggs?

3. What is the regular price for a dozen eggs?

4. What is the regular price for Lowell's orange juice?

5. How can you get a better price for Lowell's orange juice?

Understanding Store Coupons

1. You are at PriceRight Supermarket on July 23. Can you use the coupons from this ad? Why or why not?

2. You are at Quality Plus Supermarket on July 17. Can you use the coupons from this ad? Why or why not?

3. You are at PriceRight Supermarket on July 18. You are buying two 12-inch Frank's pizzas. Can you use the coupon from this ad? Why or why not?

4. You are at PriceRight Supermarket on July 19. You are buying a 12-oz. can of Lowell's orange juice. You do not have the coupon from this ad. What will you pay for the orange juice?

Figuring Prices

1. You want to buy one pound of red grapes and two pounds of green grapes. How much will the grapes cost?

2. You want to buy six ears of sweet corn. How much will the corn cost?

3. You want to buy two T-bone steaks. Each steak weighs one pound. How much will the steaks cost?

Comparing Prices

1. Two brands of cereal are on sale at PriceRight this week. Which brand gives you more cereal for your money?

2. The regular price for a 16-inch Frank's pizza is $4.50. The regular price for a 16-inch Italy's Best pizza is $3.00. You are buying two pizzas, and you have the coupon from this ad. Which brand will be cheaper?

Let's Learn More

Read these paragraphs about supermarkets in the United States.

Most Americans buy their food at large supermarkets. Supermarkets are popular because they are usually very **convenient.** Many supermarkets are open twenty-four hours a day, seven days a week. They offer a wide variety of products and services. Most supermarkets have large parking lots, so shoppers can easily park close to the store. Also, many supermarkets are located in shopping centers, so shoppers can buy food and other items in one shopping trip.

Most Americans shop for food about once a week. They usually buy a lot of food at the supermarket and then freeze or **store** it at home until they are ready to use it.

Today most U.S. supermarkets have **computer scanners** at the checkout counters. These scanners "read" the product name and price from a label on every item. Customers get a receipt showing the names and prices of all the items they buy.

U.S. supermarkets often have sales. The stores advertise their sale prices in newspapers, on television, and through the mail. Many shoppers save money by using coupons that are **distributed** by stores and **manufacturers.** Some supermarkets even give customers two or three times the value of manufacturers' coupons. By using coupons and watching for sales on products they use, Americans try to get more for their money at the supermarket.

Vocabulary Check

Study these words and their meanings.

computer scanner   (n) a machine that can "read" information from a special kind of label and put that information into a computer system
convenient   (adj) easy to use
to distribute   (v) to supply; to give out
manufacturer   (n) a person or company that makes something
to store   (v) to keep something until it is needed

Now find words in the reading that have these meanings.

1. supplied

2. keep in a very cold place

3. a paper that tells what you bought and how much you paid for it

4. easy to use

5. pieces of paper that give you a certain amount off the price of an item

Comprehension Check

Choose the best answer for each question.

1. Why are supermarkets so popular in the United States?

   a. They're coupons.   c. They're computers.
   b. They're convenient.

2. How often do most Americans go food shopping?

   a. about once a day   c. about once a month
   b. about once a week

3. When are most supermarkets open in the United States?

   a. two to four hours a day, seven days a week
   b. seven hours a day, two to four days a week
   c. twenty-four hours a day, seven days a week

4. How can American shoppers save money at the supermarket?

   a. by using coupons
   b. by buying items when they're on sale
   c. both (a) and (b)

Extension Activity

What do you think about when you're shopping for food? Most people think about the prices of the products they want to buy. Many people think about their health, too. They try to choose foods that are good for their bodies.

However, there is something else we should all think about at the supermarket: our world. Here are some things we can do at the supermarket to help our world:
1. Buy products that don't have a lot of packaging.
2. Buy food for many days in one trip to the store.
3. Buy products that come in recyclable containers (like glass bottles and aluminum cans). Then recycle them!

Talk about these ideas with your class. How can they help our world? What problems can they help to solve?

Now work with a partner to think of two other things people can do at the supermarket to help our world.

Write all the ideas on the board. Then vote on which ideas are the most important. Each student can vote for three ideas. Make a list of the three winning ideas. Take home a copy of the list and talk about the ideas with your family.

Chapter 8
At a Fast-Food Restaurant
Warm-Up

❏ Do you like to eat in fast-food restaurants? Why or why not?

❏ When do you eat in fast-food restaurants?

Words to Know

A. Here are the names of some things you can find at a fast-food restaurant. Look for them in the picture.

beverage	employee	soda
cashier	french fry	straw
cash register	menu	trash can
counter	napkin	tray
drive-up window	sandwich	

B. Many activities take place at a fast-food restaurant. Look for examples of these activities in the picture.

to carry	to smoke	to take out
to carry out	to sweep	to throw away
to complain	to take an order	to wait in line
to order		

C. Here are more words you can use to talk about the picture. Study these words and their meanings.

to be out of (v) to not have any more of
change (n) 1. money given to customers when they pay more than the total they owe (2) coins
engineer (n) a person who drives a train
expensive (adj) costing a lot of money
fillet (n) a piece of fish or meat without bones

flavor (n) what something tastes like
(food) for here (adj) food to eat in a restaurant
(food) to go (adj) food to take out of a restaurant and eat somewhere else
meal (n) food eaten at a certain time of day
mess (n) something that is dirty or not organized
shake (n) milkshake; a drink made by shaking together milk, ice cream, and a flavor (such as chocolate)
side order (n) food that is not a main dish
total (n) the amount of money a customer must pay

Now complete these sentences with words from List C. Change the form of a word if necessary.

1. I eat three _____ a day: breakfast, lunch, and dinner.

2. The cashier asked the customer, "Is this food _____ or _____ ?"

3. My favorite ice-cream _____ are chocolate and strawberry.

4. I paid for our meal with a ten-dollar bill. My _____ was seventy-three cents.

Understanding the Picture

1. Which of these foods can you buy at the Fast Food Express?

   a. hot dogs
   b. pizza
   c. ice cream
   d. chicken sandwiches
   e. salads
   f. iced tea
   g. hamburgers
   h. tacos

2. There are many employees at the Fast Food Express. Which of these jobs are they doing?

   a. taking orders
   b. throwing away trash
   c. giving children balloons
   d. washing windows
   e. cooking food
   f. parking cars

SANDWICHES
HAMBURGER 2.29
CHEESEBURGER 2.59
FISH FILLET 2.49
CHICKEN WICH 2.59
HOT DOG 2.09

BEVERAGES
SODA SM. .89 LGE. 1.05
MILK .89 COFFEE .90

SIDE ORDERS
FRENCH FRIES 1.09
ICE CREAM CONE 1.05
SHAKE 1.75

Casey Jones Special 4.99

REST ROOMS

3. Look at the menu for the Fast Food Express. Answer these questions.

a. Which items are the most expensive?
b. Which items are the least expensive?
c. How much does a hamburger cost?
d. How much does a large soda cost?
e. Which items cost less than one dollar?

4. Find the place in the picture where you can do each of these things.

a. order food from your car
b. pay for food from your car
c. receive food in your car
d. park your car while you eat inside
e. get napkins and straws
f. throw away trash
g. wash your hands

What Do You See?

Study this part of the picture. Then answer the questions.

1. What are the employees doing?

2. What are the woman in the red dress and the man in the wheelchair doing?

3. Why is the man in the suit angry?

4. Who is entering the restaurant?

5. What is the woman in the blue-green blouse doing?

What Are They Saying?

The woman in the blue-green blouse is talking to the cashier. Practice their conversation with a partner.

CASHIER: May I help you?

WOMAN: Yes. Do you have salads?

CASHIER: No, ma'am, we don't.

WOMAN: Okay. Then I'll have a fish fillet and a cup of coffee.

CASHIER: Is that for here or to go?

WOMAN: To go, please.

CASHIER: Would you like any french fries?

WOMAN: Oh, dear. They do smell good. I guess I'll have some.

CASHIER: Will that be all?

WOMAN: Yes.

CASHIER: Your total is $4.79. *(pause)* Out of five, your change is twenty-one cents.

WOMAN: Thank you.

CASHIER: And here's your food. Enjoy your meal.

WOMAN: Thanks. I will.

Now work with your partner to change the conversation so that

• The woman wants to buy a chicken sandwich instead of a salad.
• The woman doesn't want any french fries.
• The total bill is $3.63.
• The woman gives the cashier four dollars.
• The woman wants to eat her food in the restaurant.

Practice your new conversation together.

What Will Happen Next?

Answer these questions in small groups. Then compare your answers with those of the other groups.

1. What will the man in the suit do next?

2. What will the white-haired man do next?

3. What will the woman in the blue-green blouse do after she gets her food?

What Would You Say?

Act out this situation with a partner. Take turns playing parts A and B.

A. You are ordering lunch at the Fast Food Express. You want to buy a fish fillet and milk.

B. You are a cashier at the Fast Food Express. You are out of fish fillets.

What Do You See?

Study this part of the picture. Then answer the questions.

1. Why are the man in the green shirt and the woman in the white blouse unhappy?

2. Is smoking permitted in this restaurant? How can you tell?

3. What are the people in the car doing?

4. What is the dog doing?

5. What is the man in the purple shirt doing?

What Are They Saying?

The man in the car is talking to the employee at the drive-up window. Practice their conversation with a partner.

EMPLOYEE: Your total is $9.42, sir.

MAN: Okay. But can I get two shakes, too?

EMPLOYEE: Sure. What flavors do you want?

MAN: One chocolate and one vanilla.

EMPLOYEE: Just a minute. (pause) That brings your total to $13.07.

MAN: Here's fifteen dollars.

EMPLOYEE: Okay. Your change is $1.93, and here's your food. Do you need anything else?

MAN: May I have some catsup and extra napkins?

EMPLOYEE: Yes, sir. Here you are.

MAN: Thank you very much.

Now work with your partner to change the conversation so that

- The man wants a hot dog instead of two shakes.
- The man's new total is $11.64.
- The man gives the employee twelve dollars.
- The man asks for mustard instead of catsup and napkins.

Practice your new conversation together.

What Will Happen Next?

Answer these questions in small groups. Then compare your answers with those of the other groups.

1. What will happen to the man in the purple shirt?

2. What will the people in the car do next?

3. What will happen to the two men who are smoking?

What Would You Say?

Act out this situation with a partner. Take turns playing parts A and B.

A. You are paying for your food at the Fast Food Express drive-up window. Your total is $9.24, but you only have $9.00. You must take something off your order.

B. You are a cashier at the Fast Food Express drive-up window. You are helping a customer who doesn't have enough money to pay for his order. Many cars are waiting in line behind this car.

Let's Practice

Here is the menu for another fast-food restaurant, Bob's Bar-B-Q. Look at the menu. Then work in groups to answer the questions.

BOB'S BAR-B-Q

SANDWICHES

BARBECUED BEEF	2.39	HAMBURGER	1.59
HAM AND CHEESE	2.29	CHEESEBURGER	1.69
GRILLED CHICKEN	2.19	JUNIOR HAMBURGER	.99

SIDE ORDERS

FRENCH FRIES	SM .79	
	LRG .99	
ONION RINGS	1.09	
LETTUCE SALAD	1.29	

BEVERAGES

SODA	SM .79	LRG .99
ICED TEA	SM .69	LRG .89
LEMONADE	SM .69	LRG .89
COFFEE	.99 (free refills)	

Comparing Prices

1. What is the most expensive item on the menu?

2. Which side order is the most expensive?

3. Which sandwich is the least expensive?

4. Which is more expensive, a small soda or a large lemonade?

5. Which is less expensive, a salad or coffee?

Comparing Menus

1. What sandwiches can you buy at Bob's Bar-B-Q but not at the Fast Food Express?
2. What sandwiches can you buy at the Fast Food Express but not at Bob's Bar-B-Q?
3. Which restaurant sells ice cream?
4. Which restaurant sells onion rings?
5. Are hamburgers less expensive at Bob's Bar-B-Q or at the Fast Food Express?
6. Is a cup of coffee more expensive at Bob's Bar-B-Q or at the Fast Food Express?

Adding Money

Figure the total cost of these orders from Bob's Bar-B-Q.

Example: cheeseburger, large french fries, small iced tea

$1.69
.99
+ .69
———
$3.37

1. barbecued beef sandwich, onion rings, large soda
2. junior hamburger, small french fries, small lemonade
3. grilled chicken sandwich, salad, coffee

Subtracting Money

Figure how much change you should get.

Example: The total cost of your order is $4.79. You give the cashier a five-dollar bill. How much change should you get?

$5.00
-4.79
———
.21

1. The total cost of your order is $11.18. You give the cashier twelve dollars. How much change should you get?
2. The total cost of your order is $3.54. You give the cashier five dollars. How much change should you get?
3. The total cost of your order is $7.05. You give the cashier $10.05. How much change should you get?

Let's Learn More

Read these paragraphs about U.S. fast-food restaurants.

Fast-food restaurants are a **familiar** sight in almost every city and town in the United States. The first fast-food restaurants sold only a few kinds of foods. For example, when the first McDonald's opened in 1948, its menu had only five items: hamburgers, cheeseburgers, french fries, shakes, and sodas. Today, most fast-food restaurants sell a wide variety of items. Hamburgers, pizza, chicken, beef sandwiches, tacos, **submarine sandwiches**, pancakes, eggs, and more are available for a quick meal.

Many fast-food restaurants are part of large nationwide **chains**. This is why you will find restaurants that look the same and serve the same food all over the United States. Many American fast-food chains now have restaurants in other countries, too. The four biggest fast-food chains are McDonald's, Pizza Hut, Burger King, and Kentucky Fried Chicken.

Fast-food restaurants are designed to serve food quickly and **inexpensively**. Most restaurants have a menu on the wall above the counter. The customers wait in line in front of a cash register to order and pay for their food. They usually receive their food one or two minutes after ordering it. Customers can eat at tables in the restaurant or carry out their food. Many fast-food restaurants have drive-up windows, so customers can order food without leaving their cars.

Vocabulary Check

Study these words and their meanings.

chain (n) a group of businesses that are owned by the same company and have the same name
familiar (adj) well known; usual
inexpensive (adj) not costing a lot of money; cheap
submarine sandwich (n) a large sandwich made of meats and cheeses on a long bread roll

Now choose the best word to complete each sentence.

1. Jean-Luc doesn't have much money today. He needs to buy a/an _____ lunch. (familiar, inexpensive)

2. Yohei wants to eat a big meat and cheese sandwich. He will order a _____ . (submarine sandwich, hamburger)

3. — Does this restaurant serve pizza?
   — I don't know. Look at the _____ . (counter, menu)

4. This restaurant is part of a _____ . There are many other restaurants just like it. (chain, line)

Comprehension Check

Decide whether each sentence is true or false. If a sentence is false, change it to make it true.

1. McDonald's, Pizza Hut, Burger King, and Kentucky Fried Chicken are the four largest fast-food chains.

2. The first McDonald's opened in 1978.

3. Some fast-food restaurants sell breakfast foods.

Answer each question in a complete sentence.

1. How are today's fast-food restaurants different from the first American fast-food restaurants?

2. What is the purpose of a fast-food restaurant?

3. Why do we see fast-food restaurants that look the same all over the United States?

Extension Activity

Use this survey to find out which fast-food restaurant in your city is your class's favorite. Each student in the class should answer the questions. Put the results of the survey on the blackboard.

1. What is your favorite fast-food restaurant in this city? (Tell the name and location of the restaurant.)

2. Why do you like this restaurant? Choose the most important reason.
   ☐ The food is good.
   ☐ The employees are polite and helpful.
   ☐ The restaurant is clean.
   ☐ The location is convenient for me.
   ☐ The food is inexpensive.
   ☐ The food is served quickly.

3. Give the restaurant a grade for each area listed in number two. (A = excellent, B = good, C = fair, D = poor, F = unacceptable)

4. If you could change one thing about this restaurant, what would you change?

Talk about the results of your survey. Then write a class letter to the manager of the most popular restaurant. Tell about the results of your survey. Mail the letter or deliver it during a class trip to the restaurant.

Chapter 9
Emergency Services

Warm-Up

❑ What is an emergency?

❑ What are some ways that fires can start?

Words to Know

A. Here are the names of some things you can find near a fire or other emergency. Look for them in the picture.

ambulance	helmet	smoke
fire engine	hose	spectator
fire fighter	ladder	stretcher
fire hydrant	paramedic	television crew
flame	police car	
helicopter	police officer	

B. Many activities take place when there is a fire or other emergency. Look for examples of these activities in the picture.

to carry	to hurry	to shout
to climb	to point	to spray
to help	to rescue	to watch

C. Here are more words you can use to talk about the picture. Study these words and their meanings.

to be trapped   (v) to be unable to leave or move
dalmatian   (n) a kind of white dog with black spots, sometimes kept by fire departments
to escape   (v) to get away safely
fire alarm   (n) a loud bell or other noise that tells people there is a fire in a building
fire chief   (n) the person who is in charge of a fire department

to get tangled up in   (v) to get caught in
ladder truck   (n) a fire truck with big ladders
megaphone   (n) a device that makes a person's voice sound louder
to pump   (v) to pull water or another liquid out of a pipe or tank with a machine called a pump
pumper   (n) a fire truck that has a lot of hose and a pump for pulling water out of fire hydrants
roadblock   (n) something that stops people from going on a certain road
SCBA   (n) Self-Contained Breathing Apparatus; the face mask and air tank that fire fighters wear
snorkel truck   (n) a fire truck with a bucket that moves up and down for people to ride in
turnout gear   (n) the fireproof suit that a fire fighter wears

Now complete these sentences with words from Lists A and C. Change the form of a word if necessary.

1. The fire fighter put on his _____ and _____ before he went into the burning building.

2. A _____ provides emergency health care.

3. An _____ is a special truck that takes people who are sick or hurt to the hospital.

4. A person who is watching something is a _____ .

Understanding the Picture

1. Find the object in each line that is **not** in the picture.

   a. police car, ambulance, airplane, fire truck
   b. hose, ladder, fire hydrant, fire pole
   c. fog, smoke, flames, water
   d. turnout gear, SCBA, crown, helmet

2. Many of the people in this picture are watching the burning building. Find a spectator who is showing each of these feelings.

a. surprised	d. interested
b. worried	e. sad
c. afraid	f. happy

   Why do you think each spectator has this feeling?

3. Many of the people in this picture are working.
   Match each person with the job he or she is doing.

   a. paramedic   asking people questions about the fire
   b. fire fighter   helping people who were hurt in the fire
   c. fire chief   keeping spectators away from the fire
   d. television reporter   flying a helicopter to rescue people from the fire
   e. helicopter pilot   telling the fire fighters what to do
   f. police officer   putting out the fire

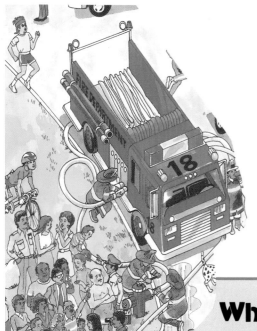

What Do You See?

Study this part of the picture. Then answer the questions.

1. What are the fire fighters doing with the fire hydrant?

2. What is the TV crew doing?

3. What are the police officers doing?

4. Why is the man by the fire hydrant wearing a towel?

5. What is the young man in the yellow shirt and red shorts doing?

What Are They Saying?

Two of the spectators are talking to each other. Practice their conversation with a partner.

SPECTATOR 1: What happened, Sonya? I just came home from the store.

SPECTATOR 2: Oh, Lydia! I'm so glad to see you. I was afraid you were trapped in your apartment. Where are your kids?

SPECTATOR 1: They're at the zoo with my mother.

SPECTATOR 2: Oh, good. You're all safe!

SPECTATOR 1: When did this start? How did it start?

SPECTATOR 2: The fire alarm went off around 11:30. Sam and I ran downstairs, and Mr. Harrison told us to leave the building.

SPECTATOR 1: Do you know how the fire started?

SPECTATOR 2: No. Some people think it started in the Wangs' apartment. They're on vacation.

SPECTATOR 1: This is awful! What should we do?

SPECTATOR 2: All we can do now is watch and wait.

Now work with your partner to change the conversation so that

- Spectator 1 just came home from a doctor's appointment.
- Spectator 2 asks Spectator 1 where her roommate is.
- Spectator 1's roommate is at work.
- Spectator 2 says that the fire alarm went off around 2:00. She thinks the fire started on the fourth floor.

Practice your new conversation together.

What Will Happen Next?

Answer these questions in small groups. Then compare your answers with those of the other groups.

1. What will the TV crew do next?

2. What will happen to the man who is wearing the towel?

3. What will the young man in the yellow shirt and red shorts do next?

What Would You Say?

Act out this situation in groups of three. Take turns playing parts A, B, and C.

A. You are watching your home burn. Fire fighters are trying to put out the fire. You were at home alone when you smelled smoke and found the fire. You ran to your neighbor's house to call the fire department.

B. You are watching your neighbor's house burn. Fire fighters are trying to put out the fire. You are trying to help your neighbor.

C. You just got home from work. Your neighbor's house is burning. You want to know what happened. You want to know if everyone is safe.

What Do You See?

Study this part of the picture. Then answer the questions.

1. What is the fire fighter doing on the ladder?

2. What are the people on the roof doing?

3. What is the fire chief doing with his megaphone?

4. What are the paramedics doing?

5. What is the fire fighter in the bucket doing?

What Are They Saying?

The fire fighter in the bucket is talking to the woman in the blue dress. Practice their conversation with a partner.

FIRE FIGHTER: I have you! Be careful of the glass.

WOMAN: Thank you, thank you! You saved my life!

FIRE FIGHTER: Is anyone else in your apartment?

WOMAN: No, but I think Mrs. Green is still next door. I heard her yelling a few minutes ago.

FIRE FIGHTER: Which apartment is hers?

WOMAN: That one, with the blue curtains.

FIRE FIGHTER: Okay, I'll look for her. Right now we're going down. Are you okay?

WOMAN: Yes. Just scared.

FIRE FIGHTER: Well, you did the right thing. We saw you waving that towel out the window.

WOMAN: I'm so glad. Thank you again for rescuing me. I'll never forget you!

Now work with your partner to change the conversation so that

- The woman thinks Mr. Hernandez is still upstairs.
- Mr. Hernandez lives in the apartment with the red curtains. His daughter lives with him.
- The woman feels a little sick.
- The fire fighter says the paramedics will help her.
- The fire fighters saw the woman waving a shirt out the window.

Practice your new conversation together.

What Will Happen Next?

Answer these questions in small groups. Then compare your answers with those of the other groups.

1. What will the paramedics do next?

2. What will happen to the people on the roof?

3. What will the fire fighter in the bucket do next?

What Would You Say?

Act out this situation with a partner. Take turns playing parts A and B.

A. You are a fire fighter. You are rescuing a child from the window of a burning house. You ask the child if anyone else is inside. Then you ask if she is okay.

B. You are a child in a burning house. A fire fighter is rescuing you from a window. Your parents aren't home. You think your brothers are still in the house. They might be in their bedroom.

Let's Practice

It's important to know how to escape from a fire in your home. You should have two **escape routes** (ways to escape) from every room in your home. Never use an elevator in an escape route.

Look at the floor plan for this house. With a partner, find two escape routes from every room of the house.

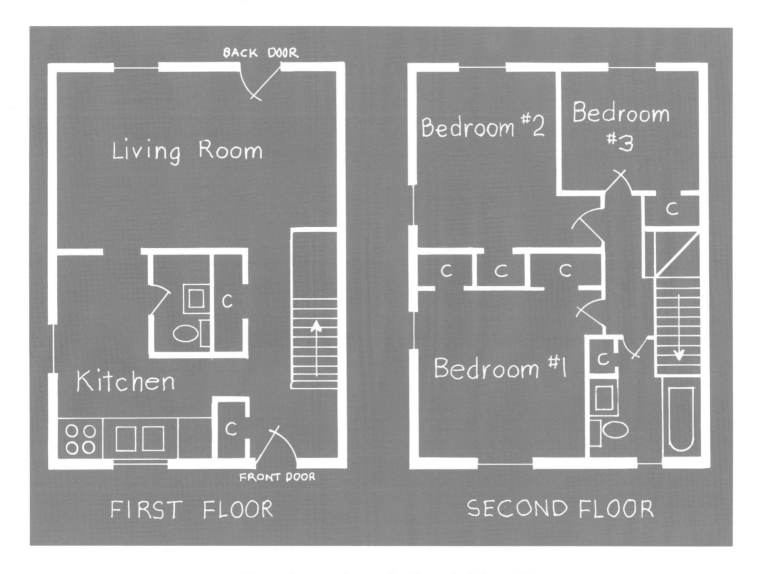

You can't escape from a fire if you don't know it's there. A **smoke detector** can "smell" smoke before you can, especially if you are asleep. It will make a loud noise to wake you up and tell you there is a fire. It's important to have a smoke detector on every floor of your home and by every bedroom. With your partner, decide where to put smoke detectors in this house.

Now make a floor plan for *your* home on a piece of paper. Find two escape routes from every room. Mark the best places for smoke detectors. Then show your partner the floor plan and talk about your escape routes.

Take your floor plan home and show it to your family. Talk about the escape routes together. Make sure you have smoke detectors in the best places. Choose a place outside your home for everyone to meet if there is a fire in your home.

Let's Learn More

Read these paragraphs about emergency services and safety in the United States.

In the United States, people can get help during an emergency by calling a fire department, police department, or ambulance. These services are paid for by tax money and are available to everyone.

The police department's job is to **enforce** the laws and to protect people from those who break the laws. The fire department puts out fires and rescues people who are in **danger.** Paramedics go out in ambulances to provide emergency health care and take people who are sick or hurt to the hospital as quickly as possible.

Every U.S. city and town has special telephone numbers that people can call to **report** emergencies and ask for help. In many cities and towns, 9-1-1 is the special emergency number. When calling to report an emergency, people must remember to tell *who* they are, *where* they are, and *what* the problem is.

U.S. police departments and fire departments also work to teach people how to stay safe and healthy. Fire fighters often visit schools to talk about fire safety and **prevention.** They teach students not to run if their clothes are on fire: instead, they should "stop, drop, and roll" on the ground to put out the fire. Police officers visit schools to talk about preventing drug and alcohol **abuse** and to help students learn about **traffic safety.**

Vocabulary Check

Study these words and their meanings.

abuse   (n) bad or wrong use; misuse
danger   (n) chance of being hurt; the opposite of safety
to enforce   (v) to make (a law) work or be followed
prevention   (n) the act of stopping something from happening
to report   (v) to tell someone about
traffic safety   (n) freedom from danger caused by cars, trucks, and other vehicles

Now find a word or phrase in List B that means the opposite of each word or phrase in List A.

A	B
1. to report	to make something happen
2. abuse	correct use
3. safety	to keep secret
4. to prevent	healthy
5. sick	danger

Comprehension Check

Choose the correct answer for each question. Each question may have one, two, three, or four correct answers.

1. Which of these things do fire fighters do?

   a. put out fires   c. buy tax money
   b. rescue people from danger d. visit schools

2. Which of these things should you say when you report an emergency?

   a. what the problem is   c. when you'll be home

   b. where you are   d. who you are

3. Which of these things do paramedics do?

   a. put out fires
   b. help people who are sick or hurt
   c. drive police cars
   d. take people to the hospital

4. Which of these things do police officers do?

   a. teach students about traffic safety
   b. protect people
   c. put out fires
   d. enforce the laws

Extension Activity

In groups of three or four, make posters to teach people about fire safety or fire prevention. Choose one of these titles for your poster:

- Ways to Prevent Fires
- Being Prepared for a Fire
- What to Do in a Fire

Use words and pictures on your poster. Show your poster to the rest of the class and talk about what it means. Answer any questions about your poster. Display all the posters in your classroom.

Unit Three
On the Go

Americans are always "on the go"—moving from one place to another. Since they own about forty percent of the world's cars, they do a lot of driving. However, many Americans use airplanes, trains, and buses when they are traveling long distances.

Chapter 10: At the Service Station shows what it's like to own a car in the United States. You will learn and practice the language you need to buy gas, get a car repaired, and use a road map.

Chapter 11: At the Bus Station, Chapter 12: At the Train Station, and **Chapter 13: At the Airport** focus on three different ways to travel long distances in the United States. These chapters provide travel information and practice in reading schedules and buying tickets.

Chapter 14: At a Motel ends this unit with a look at where Americans stay when they're away from home. You will learn about the services that are available and talk about what people do at a typical American motel. You will also learn and practice the language you need to check in or out of a motel.

Chapter 10
At the Service Station

Warm-Up

❏ What are some advantages of owning a car? What are some disadvantages of owning a car?

❏ What can you do at a service station?

Words to Know

A. Here are the names of some things you can find at a service station. Look for them in the picture.

attendant	gas pump	tow truck
car wash	jack (tool)	
flat tire	mechanic	

B. Here are the names of some parts of a car. Look for them in the picture.

antenna	headlight	steering wheel
bumper	hood	sunroof
dashboard	hubcap	tire
engine	license plate	trunk
fender	seat	windshield

C. Here are some other words you can use to talk about the picture. Study these words and their meanings.

to break down (v) to stop working or moving
to change a tire (v) to take off one tire and put on another one
chauffeur (n) a person whose job is to drive a car
to check the oil (v) to see how much oil is in a car
dinosaur (n) a very large reptile that lived millions of years ago
dolly (n) a low platform on wheels

to fill up (a car) (v) to fill the gas tank of a car with gasoline
gas station (n) service station; a place to buy gasoline
jeep (n) a car that can travel on rough ground
limousine (n) a large, comfortable car, usually driven by a chauffeur
to pump gas (v) to use the hose on a gas pump to put gasoline in a car's gas tank
to run out of gas (v) to use up all the gas in a car's gas tank
station wagon (n) an automobile with a rear door and a storage area in the back

Now complete these sentences with words from List C. Change the form of a word if necessary.

1. Jon _____ on his way to work today. He forgot to _____ his car last night.

2. My parents bought a new car. They got a _____ so they can carry many things.

3. Be sure to _____ in your car when you buy gas.

4. _____ lived and died millions of years ago.

Understanding the Picture

1. Which of these vehicles do you see at this gas station?

a. limousine	e. jeep
b. van	f. motorcycle
c. bus	g. sports car
d. tow truck	h. bicycle

2. There are many attendants at this service station. Which of these jobs are they doing?

a. using the rest room	e. driving a car
b. changing a tire	f. cleaning a windshield
c. fixing a car	g. drying a car
d. pumping gas	

3. You can buy two kinds of gas at this gas station: **regular** and **premium.** You can pump your own gas at a **self-service** pump or have an attendant pump it at a **full-service** pump. Read the signs above the gas pumps. Then answer these questions.

a. How much does a gallon of regular gas cost at the self-service pump?

b. How much does a gallon of premium gas cost at the full-service pump?

c. Which is cheaper, self-service regular or full-service regular?

d. Which is cheaper, full-service regular or full-service premium?

e. What is the cheapest gas you can buy at this gas station?

f. What is the most expensive gas you can buy at this gas station?

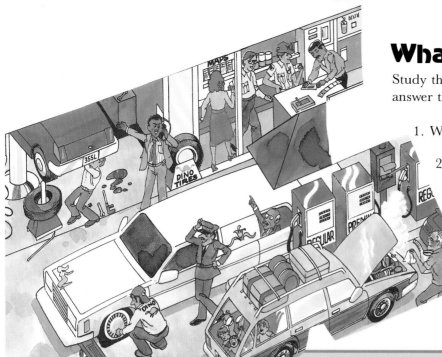

What Do You See?

Study this part of the picture. Then answer the questions.

1. What is the man in the purple shirt doing?

2. Who is the man with the blue hat? What is he doing?

3. What is the man with the purple tie doing? What is he saying?

4. What is happening inside the service station office?

5. What can you buy inside the service station office?

What Are They Saying?

The woman in the bright pink skirt is talking to the gas station attendant. Practice their conversation with a partner.

ATTENDANT: May I help you?

WOMAN: I'm here to pick up my car. I brought it in this morning for an oil change.

ATTENDANT: Okay. What's your last name?

WOMAN: Delgado.

ATTENDANT: A 1989 Ford Escort?

WOMAN: Yes, that's it.

ATTENDANT: It's all ready. That'll be $22.95.

WOMAN: May I pay for it with a credit card?

ATTENDANT: Sure. *(pause)* Sign here, please.

WOMAN: Did the mechanic look at the brakes?

ATTENDANT: Yes. He didn't see any problem with them.

WOMAN: Great! Where is my car?

ATTENDANT: It's behind the building. Here's your key.

WOMAN: Thanks a lot. Good-bye.

Now work with your partner to change the conversation so that

- The woman brought her car in for a tune-up.
- Her car is a 1991 Toyota Corolla.
- A tune-up costs $65.
- The woman's car is beside the building.

Practice your new conversation together.

What Will Happen Next?

Answer these questions in small groups. Then compare your answers with those of the other groups.

1. What will the man with the purple tie do next?

2. What will the man in the purple shirt do next?

3. What will the man inside the limousine do next?

What Would You Say?

Act out this situation with a partner. Take turns playing parts A and B.

A. You took your car to the gas station this morning because it was leaking oil. The mechanic told you to pick up your car after 4:00. It's 5:00 now, but the attendant says your car isn't ready.

B. You are a gas station attendant. A customer is here to pick up a car, but the car isn't ready yet. The mechanic says it will be ready tomorrow afternoon. You must tell the customer why the car isn't ready.

What Do You See?

Study this part of the picture. Then answer the questions.

1. What is the man in the orange shirt and green pants doing?
2. What is happening to the blue-green car at the left?
3. What is the young man with the yellow hat doing?
4. What is the driver of the tow truck doing?
5. What are the young people doing by the jeep?

What Are They Saying?

The man in the orange shirt is talking to the gas station attendant. Practice their conversation with a partner.

ATTENDANT: Do you need some directions, sir?

MAN: I think so. I'm looking for Highway 39.

ATTENDANT: There's no Highway 39 around here.

MAN: My nephew told me to take Highway 62 to Highway 39.

ATTENDANT: Where are you going?

MAN: To Riverview.

ATTENDANT: That's about fifty miles north of here.

MAN: Oh, here it is on the map.

ATTENDANT: Right. Stay on Highway 62 until you get to Highway 49. Go west on 49 for about five miles, and you'll be in Riverview.

MAN: Highway 49? I guess I wrote down the wrong number.

ATTENDANT: Or maybe your nephew gave you the wrong information!

Now work with your partner to change the conversation so that

- The man asks the attendant to give him directions.
- The man is going to Mooresville.
- Mooresville is about twenty miles west of here.
- The attendant tells the man to stay on Highway 62 until he gets to Highway 93. Then he should go north to Rock Road, and west a few miles to Mooresville.

Practice your new conversation together.

What Will Happen Next?

Answer these questions in small groups. Then compare your answers with those of the other groups.

1. What will the driver of the tow truck do next?
2. What will happen to the young people by the jeep?
3. What will the man with the map do next?

What Would You Say?

Act out this situation with a partner. Take turns playing parts A and B.

A. You are driving a long distance to visit relatives. You have a headache, so you want to buy some aspirin. You stop at a gas station and ask an attendant for directions to a drugstore.

B. You are a gas station attendant. A customer asks for directions to a drugstore. You know that there is a drugstore about a mile away, on King George Avenue. You tell the customer how to get to the drugstore.

Let's Practice

A road map shows which way the roads go in a certain area. Most road maps also show the distance between cities. When you know the distance between two cities, you can figure out how long it will take to drive from one to the other.

Look at this simplified map of Illinois. The red numbers tell the distance between the cities, in miles. (A mile equals 1.6 kilometers.) The blue numbers are the highway numbers.

Now use the map to answer these questions.

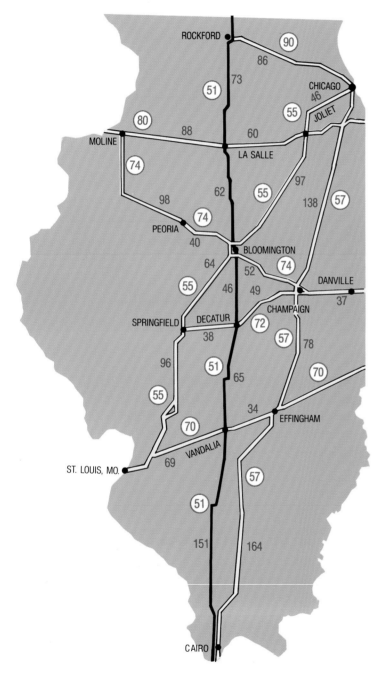

Figuring Distances

1. How far is it from
   a. Rockford to La Salle?
   b. Moline to Peoria?
   c. Chicago to Joliet?
   d. Springfield to St. Louis?
   e. Effingham to Cairo?

2. Which distance is the greatest:
   • Peoria to Bloomington,
   • Chicago to Rockford, or
   • Decatur to Vandalia?

3. How far is it from
   a. Rockford to Decatur?
   b. St. Louis to Effingham?
   c. Moline to Danville?

Figuring Travel Times

To figure out how long it will take to drive somewhere, divide the distance you will travel by the speed you will drive. In the United States, driving speeds are measured in miles per hour (mph). On most U.S. interstate highways, the speed limit is 65 mph (about 104 kilometers per hour).

Example: Traveling at 65 mph, how long will it take to drive from Effingham to Cairo?

$$\frac{164 \text{ miles}}{65 \text{ mph}} = 2.52 \text{ hours (2 hours and 31 minutes)}$$

[NOTE: .52 hours × 60 = 31.2 minutes]

1. Traveling at 65 mph, how long will it take to drive from
   a. Effingham to Champaign?
   b. Joliet to Bloomington?
   c. Rockford to Vandalia?

2. This map shows two ways to drive from Chicago to Decatur:
   • Highway 57 from Chicago to Champaign, then Highway 72 to Decatur
   • Highway 55 from Chicago to Bloomington, then Highway 51 to Decatur

   a. How long (in miles) is each trip?
   b. Traveling at 65 mph, how long will each trip take?

Let's Learn More

Read these paragraphs about American service stations.

There are more than 100,000 service stations in the United States. This large number is not surprising, because Americans own more than 130 million cars—about forty percent of the world's cars.

Most service stations do more than just sell gasoline. At a traditional service station, attendants can change the oil and mechanics can repair customers' cars. Some stations have **towing** services, too. A few stations have car washes. Most stations have public rest rooms and **vending machines.**

Today, many gas stations do not provide repair services. Instead, they often have small **convenience stores.** These gas stations are an example of the "one-stop shopping" that is so popular in the United States. A customer can fill up his car with gas and buy a frozen pizza for dinner in one stop!

In the past, all American gas stations provided "full service." Attendants pumped gas, checked the oil, and washed the windshield of every car. Today, most gas stations have **self-service pumps.** In fact, many gas stations now have *only* self-service pumps. Customers pump their own gas and pay an attendant. The gas is cheaper than it is at a **full-service pump.** This way of saving money is very popular with both men and women. Eight out of ten American drivers regularly buy their gas at self-service pumps.

Vocabulary Check

Study these words and their meanings.

convenience store   (n) a small grocery store that is usually open twenty-four hours a day
full-service pump   (n) a pump that gas station attendants use to put gas in customers' cars
self-service pump   (n) a pump that customers use to put gas in their own cars
towing   (n) pulling; using a tow truck to move a car
vending machine   (n) a machine that sells soda, coffee, or snacks such as candy and potato chips

Now find words in the reading that have these meanings.

1. fix
2. frequently
3. less expensive
4. pulling
5. usually
6. not spending
7. help yourself at these pumps
8. someone will help you at this pump
9. people who repair machines
10. small, 24-hour grocery stores

Comprehension Check

Decide whether each sentence is true or false. If a sentence is false, change it to make it true.

1. A mechanic can repair your car at any gas station in the United States.

2. Some U.S. service stations do not have full-service pumps.

3. It is cheaper to buy gas at a full-service pump than at a self-service pump.

4. Most U.S. service stations have vending machines.

5. Most American drivers do not pump their own gas.

Extension Activity

Driving is a convenient way to travel. However, cars burn gasoline and produce gases that are bad for our world. You can help to keep our world cleaner and safer by not using a car every time you go somewhere.

A. Make a list of five places you often go by car.

B. Now find a partner. Talk about the places on your lists. Ask each other these questions about each place:
   1. What other way(s) could you get to this place?
   2. How often do you go to this place?
   3. How often do you really need to go to this place?
   4. Could you travel to this place with another person who goes there?

C. Choose two things you can do to avoid (stay away from) using a car. Write them down and read them to your partner.

D. Try to do those two things during the next week. Then talk to your partner again. Did you do both things? Why or why not? How many car trips did you avoid?

Chapter 11
At the Bus Station

Warm-Up

❏ Did you ever take a long bus trip? If so, where did you go? Tell about your trip.

❏ What can you do at a bus station?

Words to Know

A. Here are the names of some things you can find at a bus station. Look for them in the picture.

arrival board	loudspeaker
baggage	luggage
baggage check-in counter	pay phone
carry-on bag	security guard
departure board	suitcase
information booth	ticket agent
locker	ticket window
lost and found department	vending machine

B. Here are some other words you can use to talk about traveling by bus. Study these words and their meanings.

A.M. (adj) before noon

arrival (n) someone or something that is arriving

baggage compartment (n) a space in the bottom of a bus to put checked bags

to board (v) to get on (a bus)

to cancel (v) to stop; to call off

departure (n) something (a bus) that is leaving

destination (n) the place to which someone or something is going

to miss (a bus) (v) to not get on a bus that one wanted to ride

one-way ticket (n) a ticket that lets you travel from one place to another, but not back again

on time (adj) at the right time; not early or late

passenger (n) someone who is traveling by bus, train, airplane, or ship

P.M. (adj) after noon

round-trip ticket (n) a ticket that lets you travel from one place to another and then back again

schedule (n) a list that tells when buses will arrive and depart; a timetable

timetable (n) a list that tells when buses will arrive and depart; a schedule

C. Here are more words you can use to talk about the objects and activities in the picture.

animal carrier	musician	soldier
broom	sailor	stroller
to check a bag	to shrug one's	to sweep
duffel bag	shoulders	to wait in line
escalator	snack bar	

Now complete these sentences with words from Lists A, B, and C. Change the form of a word if necessary.

1. —Are you waiting for the bus to Ft. Wayne?
   —Yes. What's your _____ ?

2. Andy found a watch on the floor at the bus station. He took it to the _____ .

3. Two names for a traveler's bags are _____ and _____ .

4. —When is Yolanda going to Detroit?
   —She _____ her bus today, so she's going tomorrow.

Understanding the Picture

1. Many of the people at this bus station are waiting to get on a bus. Which of these things are they doing while they wait?

   a. reading a book   e. sleeping
   b. playing basketball   f. making a telephone call
   c. watching television   g. taking pictures
   d. having a snack   h. sewing

2. There are many employees at this bus station. Which of these jobs are they doing?

   a. vacuuming the floor   e. watching people
   b. putting luggage on buses   f. taking pictures
   c. selling tickets   g. waiting in line
   d. taking passengers' luggage   h. sweeping the floor

3. Look at the departure and arrival boards in the picture. Answer these questions.

   a. What time does the bus to Ft. Wayne leave?
   b. What time did the bus from St. Louis arrive?
   c. It is 1:35 P.M. You are waiting for your friend to arrive from Iowa City. How long will you wait?
   d. You are going to Detroit. You want to be at the station a half hour before your bus leaves. What time should you get to the bus station?

4. Find the place(s) in the picture where you can do each of these things.

   a. buy something to drink
   b. get on a bus
   c. buy a bus ticket
   d. ask a question
   e. check your suitcase
   f. look for your lost keys
   g. store your luggage for a short time

What Do You See?

Study this part of the picture. Then answer the questions.

1. What is happening on the "down" escalator?

2. What is the female ticket agent doing?

3. What are the sailors doing?

4. Why are so many people standing between the ropes?

5. What is happening at the bottom of the "up" escalator?

What Are They Saying?

The female ticket agent is talking to the man in the brown jacket. Practice their conversation with a partner.

MAN: One round-trip ticket to Detroit, please.

TICKET AGENT: All right. That bus leaves at 2:00. Do you have any bags to check?

MAN: No. I just have a small bag and my dog.

TICKET AGENT: Your dog? I'm sorry, sir. You can't take a dog on the bus.

MAN: Why not? He's a very quiet dog, and he's in a carrier.

TICKET AGENT: I'm sorry, but no animals are allowed on the buses.

MAN: This is terrible! I don't know what to do.

TICKET AGENT: Do you want to think about it for a few minutes while I help the next customer?

MAN: No. Just cancel my ticket. If I can't take Duffer with me, I'll just stay home!

Now work with your partner to change the conversation so that

- The man wants to go to New Orleans.
- The bus to New Orleans leaves at 4:30 P.M.
- The man wants to take his cat with him.
- The ticket agent asks the man if he still wants his ticket.
- The man will find someone to keep his cat while he is gone.

Practice your new conversation together.

What Will Happen Next?

Answer these questions in small groups. Then compare your answers with those of the other groups.

1. What will the sailors do after they check their bags?

2. What will the man with the green hat do upstairs?

3. What will the musicians do next?

What Would You Say?

Act out this situation with a partner. Take turns playing parts A and B.

A. You waited in a long line to buy a bus ticket. Now you are talking to the ticket agent. You want to buy a round-trip ticket to Ft. Wayne. You have two bags to check.

B. You are a ticket agent at the bus station. A customer wants to buy a ticket for the bus to Ft. Wayne. The seats on that bus are already full. You can sell the customer a ticket for tomorrow's bus to Ft. Wayne.

What Do You See?

Study this part of the picture. Then answer the questions.

1. What are the two boys by the information booth doing?

2. What is the brown-haired woman doing at the information booth?

3. Why is the woman in the pink dress holding her arms out?

4. What is happening by the bus to Ft. Wayne?

5. What is the man in the green suit doing? How does he feel?

What Are They Saying?

The man at the information booth has a problem with his ticket. He is talking to one of the employees behind the counter. Practice their conversation with a partner.

MAN: I just bought this ticket to Ft. Wayne, but the ticket agent made a mistake.

EMPLOYEE: What's the problem?

MAN: I paid for a round-trip ticket, but he only gave me a one-way ticket. I just saw the mistake a minute ago. What should I do?

EMPLOYEE: Talk to the agent who sold you the ticket. He can give you a new one.

MAN: But look at the line! If I wait in that line again, I'll miss my bus!

EMPLOYEE: Hmmmm. Which agent helped you?

MAN: The one on the left.

EMPLOYEE: All right. Let's talk to him.

MAN: Thank you. I appreciate your help.

EMPLOYEE: No problem. I'm sorry about the mistake.

Now work with your partner to change the conversation so that

- The man paid for a ticket to Ft. Wayne, but the ticket agent gave him a ticket to Detroit.
- The agent on the right helped the man.
- The employee at the information booth will call the agent on the telephone.

Practice your new conversation together.

What Will Happen Next?

Answer these questions in small groups. Then compare your answers with those of the other groups.

1. What will happen to the two boys by the information booth?

2. What will the man in the green suit do when he gets on the bus?

3. What will the child in the stroller do next?

What Would You Say?

Act out this situation with a partner. Take turns playing parts A and B.

A. You are waiting for the bus to Detroit. You bought your ticket, but now you can't find it. You go to the information booth to see if anyone found the ticket and turned it in. You ask what you should do.

B. You are working at the bus station information booth. You have not seen this person's ticket. You tell the person he will have to buy a new ticket if he can't find it.

Let's Practice

If you want to travel by bus, you must learn to read a bus schedule. Look at this schedule for buses traveling from Pittsburgh to New York. Read **down** to follow the schedule.

PITTSBURGH—NEW YORK CITY

Bus Number		1372	1374	1378	1368	1370
Pittsburgh, PA	Lv	1 00	5 15	**12 01**	**6 15**	**11 10**
Monroeville			5 35	**12 25**	**6 40**	
Somerset				**1 35**	**7 50**	
Carlisle			9 05			
HARRISBURG, PA	Ar	5 00	9 40	**4 25**	**10 40**	3 10
	Lv	5 30	10 15	**5 15**	**11 10**	3 30
Allentown	Ar		11 55			
	Lv		**12 05**			
Bethlehem			**12 25**			
Easton			**12 50**			
King of Prussia		7 15				
PHILADELPHIA	Ar	8 05		**7 20**	1 15	5 35
	Lv	9 00		**8 00**	1 40	6 00
Bristol, PA						6 40
Camden, NJ		9 10		**8 10**		
Newark, NJ			**2 05**			
NEW YORK, NY	Ar	11 20	**2 40**	**10 20**	3 50	8 20

A.M.—Lightface type   Ar = Arrives
P.M.—Boldface type   Lv = Leaves

Work in groups to answer these questions about the bus schedule. Use A.M. and P.M. in your answers as needed.

Understanding the Schedule

1. How many buses travel from Pittsburgh to New York City each day?

2. At what times do the buses leave Pittsburgh?

3. At what times do the buses arrive in New York?

4. How many buses travel from Monroeville, PA, to New York City each day?

5. How many buses travel from Pittsburgh to Philadelphia each day?

Finding Arrival and Departure Times

1. You want to travel from Allentown, PA, to New York City. What time does the bus leave Allentown? What time does it arrive in New York City?

2. You want to travel from Harrisburg, PA, to Newark, NJ. What time does the bus leave Harrisburg? What time does it arrive in Newark?

3. You want to travel from Philadelphia to Camden, NJ, in the evening. What time does the bus leave Philadelphia? What time does it arrive in Camden?

Figuring Travel Times

1. You are taking bus number 1378 from Pittsburgh to New York City. How long will the trip take?

2. You are taking bus number 1372 from Harrisburg to Philadelphia. How long will the trip take?

3. You are taking bus number 1374 from Carlisle to Easton. How long will the trip take?

Choosing a Bus

1. You are going from Pittsburgh to Harrisburg. You want to travel in the afternoon. Which bus should you take?

2. You are going from Philadelphia to New York City. You want to travel as quickly as possible. Which bus should you take?

Let's Learn More

Read these paragraphs about traveling by bus in the United States.

Riding a bus is not the fastest way to travel long distances. However, traveling by bus has many advantages. It is the cheapest kind of long-distance transportation. Buses use less **fuel** per passenger than cars, airplanes, or trains do, so they are better for the **environment**. Also, most bus stations—unlike airports—are conveniently located in the middle of cities.

In the 1930s and 1940s, the system of **intercity** buses grew quickly in the United States. However, the use of these buses began to **decline** in the 1950s as more and more Americans bought cars. Today, buses are still a popular way to travel in the United States—especially for people who do not own cars and for people who do not live near an airport or train station. Intercity buses go to thousands of U.S. communities. Only about five hundred communities have airplane or train service.

In the United States, intercity buses carry about 333 million passengers a year. Many buses also carry mail and packages. There are about 1,500 bus companies **operating** 21,000 buses in the United States. For many years, the two largest U.S. bus companies were Greyhound and Trailways. These companies **merged** in the late 1980s. Today the company is called Greyhound Lines, Inc.

Vocabulary Check

Study these words and their meanings.

to decline (v) to go down; to decrease
environment (n) the natural world, including the air, land, and water
fuel (n) something that is burned to make energy. Gas, oil, wood, and coal are all fuels.
intercity (adj) going between cities
to merge (v) to combine; to come together
to operate (v) to make something work

Now find words in the reading that mean the opposite of these words and phrases.

1. separated
2. increase
3. most expensive
4. staying in one city
5. worse

Comprehension Check

Answer each question in a complete sentence.

1. What is the least expensive way to travel long distances in the United States?

2. Why are buses better for the environment than cars, airplanes, and trains are?

3. Why did many people stop riding buses in the 1950s?

4. How many people travel by intercity bus each year in the United States?

5. What is the name of the largest U.S. bus company?

Extension Activity

Look at the bus schedule on page 72 or another bus schedule. Plan a trip from one city to another, and choose which bus you will take. Write the names of the cities and the bus number on a piece of paper.

Find a partner. Exchange bus schedules and play "Twenty Questions" to find out (1) where your partner is leaving from, (2) where he is going, and (3) which bus he is taking. Look at your partner's bus schedule and ask him questions that can be answered with "yes" or "no," such as

1. Are you leaving from Springfield?
2. Are you going to Manchester?
3. Does your bus leave at 3:10 P.M.?
4. Does your bus stop in Louisville?
5. Are you taking bus number 123?

You may ask only twenty questions. The game ends after you ask twenty questions OR when you can tell your partner where he is leaving from, where he is going, and which bus he is taking. Then let your partner ask twenty questions to find out about your bus trip.

Chapter 12

At the Train Station

Warm-Up

❏ Do you ever travel by train? If so, tell about your favorite train trip. Why did you like it?

❏ What can people do at a train station?

Words to Know

A. Here are the names of some things you can find at a train station. Look for them in the picture.

arrival board
baggage
baggage check-in counter
carry-on bag
conductor
departure board
information booth
loudspeaker

luggage
luggage cart
pay phone
redcap
suitcase
ticket agent
ticket window
vending machine

B. Here are more words you can use to talk about trains. Study these words and their meanings.

A.M.   (adj) before noon
arrival   (n) someone or something that is arriving
to board   (v) to get on (a train)
coach   (n) a train car with seats for passengers
departure   (n) something (a train) that is leaving
destination   (n) the place to which someone or something is going
engineer   (n) the person who drives a train
freight train   (n) a train that carries goods
one-way ticket   (n) a ticket that lets you travel from one place to another, but not back again
passenger   (n) someone who is traveling by train, airplane, bus, or ship

P.M.   (adj) after noon
reservation   (n) an arrangement to use something at a certain time
round-trip ticket   (n) a ticket that lets you travel from one place to another and then back again
schedule   (n) a list that tells when trains will arrive and depart; a timetable
timetable   (n) a list that tells when trains will arrive and depart; a schedule
track   (n) the metal rails that trains move on

C. Here are some other words you can use to talk about the objects and activities in the picture.

automatic teller machine (ATM)
to be in a hurry
to check a bag
coffee shop

duffel bag
sailor
teddy bear
to wait in line

Now complete these sentences with words from Lists A, B, and C. Change the form of a word if necessary.

1. Jamila is really _____ to board the train.

2. Do you want a round-trip ticket or a _____ ?

3. Sam _____ for ten minutes to _____ his bag.

4. Julia asked a _____ to carry her bags.

Understanding the Picture

1. We can see three tracks at this train station—tracks 8, 9, and 10. Which track should you go to if you are taking the train to

   a. St. Louis?
   b. New York?
   c. Denver?
   d. Albany?
   e. Seattle?

2. Many of the people at this train station are waiting to get on a train. Which of these things are they doing while they wait?

   a. sleeping
   b. watching TV
   c. riding a skateboard
   d. eating
   e. talking on the telephone
   f. writing a letter
   g. shopping
   h. reading a newspaper

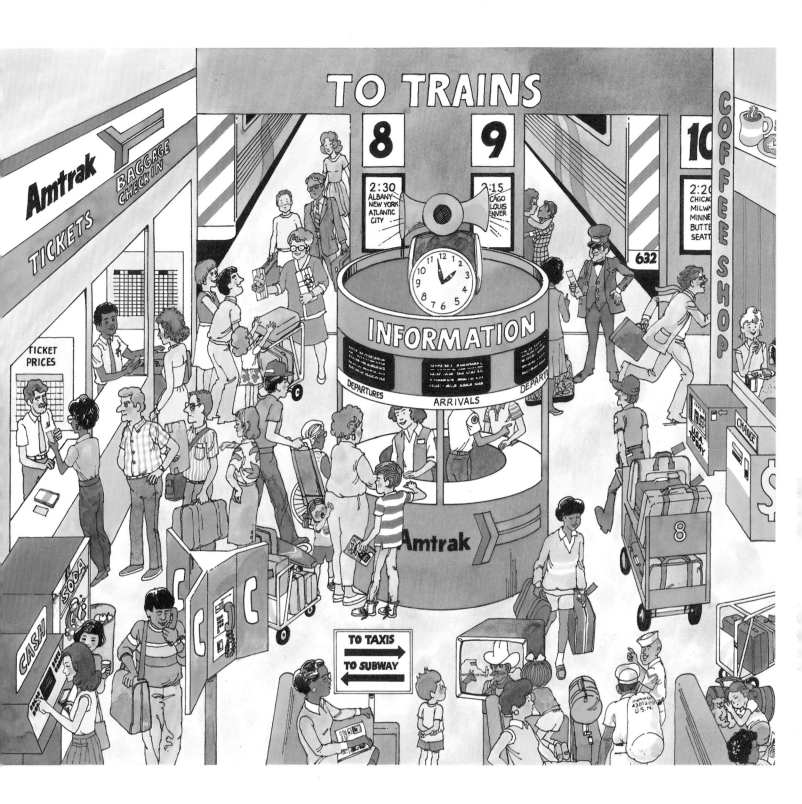

3. Find the place(s) in the picture where you can do each of these things.

a. ask a question
b. eat a snack
c. buy a train ticket
d. check your suitcase
e. get money
f. buy a soda
g. make a telephone call
h. board a train

4. Most train stations have many machines people can use. Which of these machines do you see in the picture?

a. coffee machine
b. automatic teller machine
c. stamp machine
d. newspaper machine
e. soda machine
f. change machine

What Do You See?

Study this part of the picture. Then answer the questions.

1. What is the woman in the yellow dress doing?

2. What is the woman in the pink blouse doing?

3. How does the man in the green pants feel?

4. What is the man with the glasses doing?

5. What is the woman in the purple skirt doing?
   What is she wearing on her head?

What Are They Saying?

The ticket agent is talking to the woman in the pink blouse. Practice their conversation with a partner.

TICKET AGENT: May I help you?

WOMAN: Yes. I have this ticket for next Saturday's train to St. Louis. I need to exchange it.

TICKET AGENT: Do you want to go somewhere else?

WOMAN: No. I'm still going to St. Louis, but I need to go today. My sister had her baby early!

TICKET AGENT: I see. The next train to St. Louis leaves at 2:15. Will that be all right?

WOMAN: That's fine. I'm ready to go!

TICKET AGENT: Okay. I'll get a new ticket for you. *(pause)* Here's your ticket. You can board the train now at Track 9. Do you have any bags to check?

WOMAN: No, I'll just carry them on.

TICKET AGENT: Have a nice trip.

WOMAN: Thank you.

Now work with your partner to change the conversation so that

- The woman has a ticket for the 2:15 train to St. Louis. She wants to buy another ticket for that train.
- The ticket agent asks if the ticket is for an adult.
- The ticket is for a child.
- Children under ten travel for half price.
- The price of this ticket is $28.00.

Practice your new conversation together.

What Will Happen Next?

Answer these questions in small groups. Then compare your answers with those of the other groups.

1. What will the woman in the yellow dress do after she leaves the baggage check-in counter?

2. What will happen to the woman's suitcases?

3. What will the man with the glasses do after he buys his ticket?

What Would You Say?

Act out this situation with a partner. Take turns playing parts A and B.

A. You want to take the train to Milwaukee next Thursday and return home on Sunday. You must arrive by 3:00 P.M. Thursday. You need tickets for two adults and a twelve-year-old child.

B. You are a ticket agent at the train station. You know that there are two trains to Milwaukee next Thursday. There is one train returning on Sunday. Children under ten travel for half price.

What Do You See?

Study this part of the picture. Then answer the questions.

1. What is the woman in the orange skirt doing?

2. What is the young man in the striped sweater doing?

3. What is the woman with the book doing?

4. What are the children doing?

5. Why is the sailor smiling?

What Are They Saying?

The young man using the pay phone is talking to his mother. Practice their conversation with a partner.

YOUNG MAN: Hi, Mom.

MOTHER: Richard! Where are you? You should be on the train now.

YOUNG MAN: That's why I'm calling. I'm still in Detroit. My train didn't leave on time.

MOTHER: What's the problem?

YOUNG MAN: I guess the train had some mechanical problems. I think we're going to leave here at 3:00, but I don't know when we'll get to Albany.

MOTHER: I'll call the station later to find out when your train will arrive. Don't worry, we'll be there to pick you up.

YOUNG MAN: Thanks, Mom. I can't wait to get home!

MOTHER: I'll be happy to see you, too. Have a safe trip.

Now work with your partner to change the conversation so that

• The young man missed his train.
• He got stuck in a traffic jam on his way to the train station.
• The next train to Albany leaves at 4:20. It gets to Albany at 11:30 P.M.
• His mother says she will pick him up.
• The young man is sorry that he will arrive so late.

Practice your new conversation together.

What Will Happen Next?

Answer these questions in small groups. Then compare your answers with those of the other groups.

1. What will happen to the little girl sleeping on the bench?

2. What will the woman in the orange skirt do next?

3. What will the two sailors do next?

What Would You Say?

Act out this situation with a partner. Take turns playing parts A and B.

A. You are taking the train to visit your uncle in Baltimore. When your train stops in New York, you get off and call your uncle. You tell him that the train will arrive late in Baltimore.

B. You are planning to pick up your niece at the train station this evening. She calls from New York to say that the train will arrive late in Baltimore. It is almost an hour behind schedule right now.

Let's Practice

A train schedule tells where a train goes and what time it gets to each city. This schedule is for a train called the Southwest Chief. It travels between Albuquerque, NM, and Los Angeles, CA. Read **down** on the left to learn about the trip from Albuquerque to Los Angeles, and read **up** on the right to learn about the trip from Los Angeles to Albuquerque.

SOUTHWEST CHIEF		
3 ◄——— Train Number ———► 4		
Daily ◄——— Days of Operation ———► Daily		
Read Down		*Read Up*
5 10P Dp	Albuquerque, NM	Ar 1 25P
7 31P	Gallup, NM	10 41A
8 12P	Winslow, AZ	7 58A
9 24P	Flagstaff, AZ	6 57A
12 16A	Kingman, AZ	4 03A
1 38A	Needles, CA	2 50A
4 20A	Barstow, CA	11 50P
6 15A	San Bernardino, CA	10 03P
6 50A	Pomona, CA	9 25P
7 25A	Pasadena, CA	8 55P
8 10A Ar	Los Angeles, CA	Dp 8 30P

A—A.M.	Ar = Arrives
P—P.M.	Dp = Departs

Work in groups to answer these questions about the train schedule. Use A.M. and P.M. in your answers as needed.

Understanding the Schedule

1. What is the name of this train?

2. What is the number of the train that goes from Albuquerque to Los Angeles?

3. What days do Trains 3 and 4 operate?

Using the Schedule

1. What time does Train 4 arrive in Albuquerque?

2. What time does Train 3 arrive in Los Angeles?

3. How many times does Train 3 stop between Albuquerque and Los Angeles?

Figuring Travel Times

1. You are taking Train 4 from Los Angeles to San Bernardino, CA. How long will the trip take?

2. You are taking Train 3 from Gallup, NM, to Flagstaff, AZ. How long will the trip take?

3. You are taking Train 4 from Pasadena to Needles, CA. How long will the trip take?

Learning About Services

The Southwest Chief offers these services:

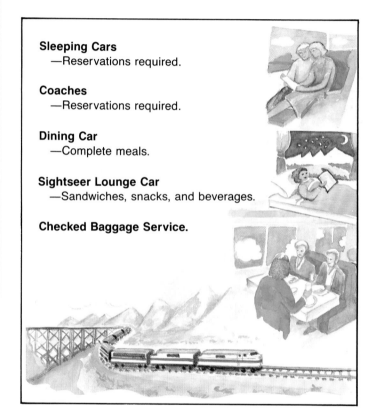

Sleeping Cars
—Reservations required.

Coaches
—Reservations required.

Dining Car
—Complete meals.

Sightseer Lounge Car
—Sandwiches, snacks, and beverages.

Checked Baggage Service.

Study the list of services and answer these questions.

1. You are going to travel from Winslow, AZ, to Los Angeles on Train 3. Do you want a reservation for a sleeping car or a coach? Explain your answer.

2. You are traveling from Flagstaff, AZ, to Gallup, NM, on Train 4. You want to eat breakfast. Where will you go? Explain your answer.

3. You are going to travel from Kingman, AZ, to Pomona, CA, on Train 3. You have three heavy suitcases. What will you do with them? Explain your answer.

Let's Learn More

Read these paragraphs about the U.S. railroad system.

Steam-powered trains appeared in the United States between 1815 and 1830. By 1835, there were more than one thousand miles of railroad track in the eastern United States. The first railroad across the American West was finished in 1869. It took people to live in this part of the country. By 1900, the United States had four more **transcontinental** railroads. For a while, trains were the fastest and easiest way to move people and **goods** across the country.

Today, other forms of transportation are more popular in the United States. Most Americans now travel long distances by car or airplane. U.S. railroads still carry a lot of goods, but most goods are now moved from one city to another by truck.

The U.S. railroad system is not controlled by the government. Most freight trains are owned and **operated** by private companies. **Intercity** passenger trains are operated by the National Railroad Passenger Corporation, called *Amtrak* (from the words *American, travel,* and *track*). The Amtrak system includes more than 20,000 miles of track. Most of its trains travel at speeds of fifty to sixty miles per hour (about eighty to ninety-five kilometers per hour).

Commuter trains are available in some **metropolitan** areas. These trains travel between a big city and its **suburbs** or nearby cities. Most commuter trains are owned and operated by local governments or private companies.

Vocabulary Check

Study these words and their meanings.

goods (n) things that can be bought, sold, and moved; freight

intercity (adj) going between cities

metropolitan (adj) having to do with a large city

to operate (v) to make something work

suburb (n) a small town or community on the edge of a big city

transcontinental (adj) going across a continent

Now find a word or phrase in List B that means the opposite of each word or phrase in List A.

A	B
1. staying in one city	freight train
2. passenger train	metropolitan
3. went away	private
4. public	intercity
5. having to do with a small town	appeared

Comprehension Check

Choose the best ending for each sentence.

1. In the United States, intercity passenger trains are operated by
   a. local governments.   b. Amtrak.

2. In some metropolitan areas, people travel to and from work by
   a. commuter train.   b. freight train.

3. The average speed of an Amtrak train is about
   a. 80 to 95 mph.   b. 50 to 60 mph.

4. The first intercontinental railroad took people to live on America's
   a. West Coast.   b. East Coast.

5. The federal government
   a. does not control the U.S. railroad system.
   b. owns and operates most trains in the United States.

Extension Activity

In groups of three or four, talk about the reasons why train travel is not as popular in the United States as it is in some other countries. Then make a list of reasons why more Americans should travel by train.

Imagine that your group is an advertising agency hired by Amtrak. Your job is to make a radio commercial that will convince people to ride Amtrak. Radio stations all over the United States will play your commercial.

Decide how you will convince people to ride Amtrak. Then prepare and practice your commercial together. If possible, make a tape recording of the commercial.

As a class, listen to all the commercials. Talk about which ones are the most convincing, and why.

Chapter 13

At the Airport

Warm-Up

❑ What do people do at an airport?

❑ Did you ever travel in an airplane? If so, where did you go?

Words to Know

A. Here are the names of some things you can find at an airport. Look for them in the picture.

airplane	departure board	metal detector
arrival board	flight attendant	security guard
baggage	information booth	suitcase
carry-on bag	luggage	ticket agent
check-in counter	luggage cart	waiting area

B. Here are some other words you can use to talk about traveling by airplane. Study these words and their meanings.

arrival (n) someone or something that is arriving

baggage claim area (n) the place where passengers can find their baggage after they get off an airplane

to board (v) to get on (an airplane)

boarding pass (n) a paper that tells a passenger's seat number for a certain flight

customs (n) a place where people's luggage is inspected when they arrive in a country

customs inspector (n) a person who looks at travelers' luggage when they arrive in a country

departure (n) something that is leaving

duty (n) a tax on something coming into a country

duty-free shop (n) a place to buy things without paying taxes

flight (n) a trip in an airplane

gate (n) a place where people leave a terminal to get on a plane or enter a terminal after getting off a plane

to land (v) to come down from the air

passenger (n) someone who is traveling by airplane, bus, train, or ship

pilot (n) someone who flies an airplane

to take off (v) to leave the ground

terminal (n) a building at an airport

C. Here are some other words you can use to talk about the objects and activities in the picture.

amplifier	luggage tag	to sniff
camera	mechanic	teddy bear
to check a bag	to meet	ten-gallon hat
fur coat	movie star	video camera
guitar	photographer	to wait
to inspect	robot	to wait in line

Now complete these sentences with words from List B. Change the form of a word if necessary.

1. You must have a _____ to get on an airplane.

2. When you fly to a different country, a _____ may inspect your bags at the airport.

3. After Joel got off the airplane, he went to the _____ to get his suitcase.

4. Vivian's _____ is leaving from _____ 14.

Understanding the Picture

1. There are many people working in this picture. Which of these jobs are they doing?

   a. inspecting bags
   b. boarding a plane
   c. giving information
   d. sniffing luggage
   e. moving luggage carts
   f. working in a shop
   g. selling tickets
   h. playing the guitar

2. Find someone in the picture who is doing each of these things.

   a. taking a picture
   b. reading a magazine
   c. asking a question
   d. waiting in line
   e. putting on a necklace
   f. fighting about a suitcase
   g. getting off an airplane
   h. working on an airplane

3. Which item in each line is **not** in the picture?

a. ticket agent, flight attendant, pilot, mechanic
b. carry-on bag, suitcase, luggage cart, shopping cart
c. baggage claim area, snack bar, customs, duty-free shop
d. cash register, metal detector, customs inspector, passenger

4. Find the place(s) in the picture where you can do each of these things.

a. wait to board an airplane
b. find your luggage
c. buy a necklace
d. learn what time a plane leaves

e. ask a question
f. buy a ticket
g. meet a visitor
h. check your bags

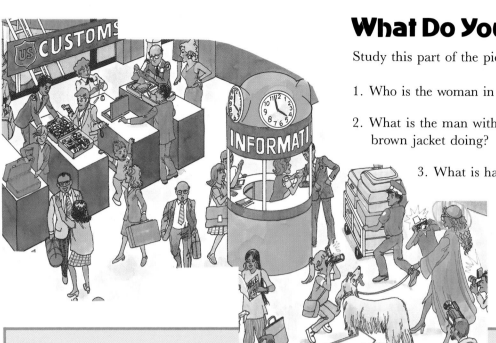

What Do You See?

Study this part of the picture. Then answer the questions.

1. Who is the woman in the pink coat? How do you know?

2. What is the man with the beard and the brown jacket doing?

3. What is happening at the information booth?

4. What is the man with the green jacket and the duffel bag doing?

5. What is the customs inspector with the glasses doing?

What Are They Saying?

The woman with the shoulder bag is talking to the employee at the information booth. Practice their conversation with a partner.

WOMAN: Excuse me. Excuse me!

EMPLOYEE: I'll be with you in just a minute. I'm almost finished helping this gentleman.

WOMAN: I can't wait! It's an emergency!

EMPLOYEE: What's the problem?

WOMAN: My son is lost. He's only five years old.

EMPLOYEE: Oh, dear. What's his name?

WOMAN: Mark Richardson.

EMPLOYEE: What is he wearing?

WOMAN: A red sweater, blue jeans, and white tennis shoes. He has blonde hair and blue eyes.

EMPLOYEE: All right. I'll read this information over the loudspeaker.

WOMAN: Please hurry! Our plane leaves in ten minutes.

Now work with your partner to change the conversation so that

- The woman's daughter is lost.
- The girl's name is Hilary Lutz.
- Hilary is wearing a purple dress and pink tennis shoes. She has brown hair and green eyes.
- The woman's plane leaves in five minutes.

Practice your new conversation together.

What Will Happen Next?

Answer these questions in small groups. Then compare your answers with those of the other groups.

1. What will the woman in the pink coat do next?

2. What will happen to the man with all the cameras?

3. What will the girl with the camera do next?

What Would You Say?

Act out this situation with a partner. Take turns playing parts A and B.

A. It is 1:20 P.M. You just got to the airport for your 1:30 flight. You run to a nearby information booth and ask where you should go to catch Eagle Flight 149.

B. You are an employee at an airport information booth. You look on the departure board to find the gate number for Eagle Flight 149. Then you tell person A to come to the airport sooner next time.

What Do You See?

Study this part of the picture. Then answer the questions.

1. What is the dog doing? Why?

2. What is happening at the metal detector?

3. What is the girl with the teddy bear doing?

4. What are the men in the baggage claim area doing?

5. What are the people in the red chairs doing?

What Are They Saying?

The girl with the teddy bear is talking to her mother and grandparents. Practice their conversation in groups of four.

MOTHER: Cindy! Here we are!

GIRL: Hi, Mom! Hi, Grandpa and Grandma! Thanks for coming to meet me at the airport.

GRANDMA: We missed you.

GRANDPA: How was your flight?

GIRL: Pretty good. I had a window seat, so I saw everything we flew over. That was pretty neat!

MOTHER: Did you have anything to eat on the plane?

GIRL: Yes. I had a chicken sandwich and a salad for lunch. But I'm still a little hungry.

GRANDMA: Well, I baked some banana bread this morning. You can have some for a snack.

GRANDPA: Did you have a good time with your dad?

GIRL: Yes, we had lots of fun. We went to the zoo and to an amusement park.

MOTHER: That's great, honey. I'm glad you had fun, but I'm happy you're home again.

Now work with your group to change the conversation so that

• The girl had an aisle seat, so she couldn't see out the window.
• The girl didn't get a meal on her flight. She's really hungry.
• They will have lunch when they get home.
• The girl had fun with her cousins. They played tennis and went swimming every day.

Practice your new conversation together.

What Will Happen Next?

Answer these questions in small groups. Then compare your answers with those of the other groups.

1. What will the security guard by the metal detector do next?

2. What will happen to the people in the red chairs?

3. What will happen to the green suitcase with the orange stripe?

What Would You Say?

Act out this situation with a partner. Take turns playing parts A and B.

A. You just flew to visit your sister. When she meets you in the terminal, you ask where her husband is. Then you tell her all about your flight.

B. You are meeting your brother at the airport. He will stay with you for a week. You are very happy to see him. You ask about his flight and talk about your plans for the week. Your husband is at work.

Let's Practice

The arrival and departure boards at an airport tell when and where each flight will take off and land. This information will help you when you want to board a plane or meet someone who is arriving on a plane.

Look at these airport arrival and departure boards. Then work with a partner to answer the questions.

WELCOME TO O'HARE INTERNATIONAL AIRPORT

ARRIVALS

AIRLINE	FLIGHT	FROM	GATE	TIME
WESTERN	292	PHOENIX	18	2:43
WESTERN	293	DALLAS	23	2:50
EAGLE	164	NEW YORK	05	2:52
EAGLE	137	ORLANDO	02	3:00
SKYWAY	608	DETROIT	14	3:10
WESTERN	288	DENVER	20	3:18
SKYWAY	611	MINNEAPOLIS	11	3:23
EAGLE	145	BOSTON	04	3:29

DEPARTURES

AIRLINE	FLIGHT	TO	GATE	TIME
EAGLE	149	NEW ORLEANS	01	2:38
SKYWAY	607	CINCINNATI	12	2:45
WESTERN	290	ST. LOUIS	22	2:51
SKYWAY	610	INDIANAPOLIS	15	2:59
WESTERN	291	PHOENIX	18	3:04
EAGLE	163	NEW YORK	05	3:11
WESTERN	295	DALLAS	23	3:17
SKYWAY	614	LOS ANGELES	13	3:21

Understanding the Arrival Board

1. What time will Flight 164 arrive at O'Hare?

2. What time will the plane from Denver arrive at O'Hare?

3. Which airline has a flight from Orlando?

4. Which flight is arriving at gate 11?

5. Which gate will the flight from Dallas arrive at?

Understanding the Departure Board

1. What time will Flight 610 leave O'Hare?

2. Where is Flight 295 going?

3. Which gate is the plane to Phoenix leaving from?

4. Which flight is leaving from gate 5?

5. Which airline has a flight to Los Angeles?

Using the Arrival and Departure Boards

1. You are flying from O'Hare to New York on Eagle Flight 163. Where should you go to board your plane? When will your plane take off?

2. You are at O'Hare Airport to meet some friends flying in from Minneapolis. Which airline are they using? Where should you go to meet them? What time will their plane arrive?

3. You see a friend at O'Hare Airport. You are flying to Indianapolis, and he is flying to Cincinnati. Whose plane will take off first? Which gate should each of you go to?

Let's Learn More

Read these paragraphs about air travel in the United States.

More than half the world's **airline** passengers are Americans. Over 400 million people a year fly from one place to another within the United States. O'Hare International Airport in Chicago is the world's busiest airport. At O'Hare, about fifty planes land and take off every hour.

Air travel is popular in the United States because it is so fast and the country is so big. For example, a **nonstop** flight from New York City to Los Angeles takes about six hours. Driving this distance nonstop would take about fifty-six hours! Traveling by airplane saves a lot of time, and most Americans **value** their time highly. Air travel is also important for international travelers. Trips that once took weeks by boat now take only a few hours by plane.

Flying can be expensive, but most U.S. airlines offer cheaper **fares** if you buy your tickets a few weeks before your flight. You can call an airline to get information and to buy a ticket. If you pay for your ticket with a credit card, the airline will mail it to you. Another way to buy plane tickets is to use a **travel agent.** Travel agents have information about all the airlines and can help you find the cheapest fare and the best flight for you. You do not have to pay a travel agent to get your tickets for you.

About 500 airports serve **commercial** airlines in the United States. Most airports provide places for passengers to eat, shop, and relax while they are waiting for their flights.

Vocabulary Check

Study these words and their meanings.

airline   (n) a company that owns and operates airplanes
commercial   (adj) meant to make money
fare   (n) the cost of riding on an airplane, bus, or train
nonstop   (adj, adv) without stopping; without interruptions
travel agent   (n) someone whose job is to arrange trips
to value   (v) to prize; to think something is worth a lot

Now choose the best word to complete each sentence.

1. Do your parents _____ education? (pay, value)

2. This is a/an _____ flight from Chicago to Miami. (nonstop, international)

3. The _____ for this flight is $379. (fare, airline)

4. Did you buy your ticket from the airline, or did you use a _____? (credit card, travel agent)

5. Flying is usually the most _____ way to travel. (commercial, expensive)

Comprehension Check

Choose the best answer for each question.

1. Why do many Americans travel by plane?
   a. because air travel is expensive
   b. because air travel is fast
   c. because air travel is nonstop

2. How can you get a cheaper fare for a flight?
   a. by using a credit card
   b. by buying your ticket a few weeks before your flight
   c. by paying a travel agent

3. What can passengers do at most airports?
   a. buy plane tickets, check baggage, and board planes
   b. eat, shop, and relax
   c. all of the above

4. Which of these sentences is not true?
   a. A travel agent has information about all the airlines.
   b. A travel agent is expensive to use.
   c. A travel agent can help you get the cheapest fare.

Extension Activity

Divide the class into two teams to play "Airline Careers."

First, each team must think of eight jobs (careers) that have to do with traveling by airplane. Write the name of each job on a small piece of paper. Put the papers in a bag.

Exchange bags with the other team. Don't look at the papers in the bag! The members of each team should stand in a line. Decide which team will start the game.

The first person on Team A pulls a paper out of her team's bag and looks at it. Without using the words on the paper, she must describe the job so that her team can guess what it is. The team has one minute to guess the job. If someone guesses the job correctly, Team A gets one point. If the student who is describing the job says one of the words on the paper, Team B gets a point. Then it's Team B's turn to guess a job.

Let a different student describe each job. Continue until both bags of careers are empty. The team with the most points wins the game.

Chapter 14

At a Motel

Warm-Up

❏ When do people go to a motel?

❏ Do you like to stay in motels?
Why or why not?

Words to Know

A. Here are the names of some things you can find at a motel. Look for them in the picture.

balcony	front desk	room key
bikini	ice machine	suitcase
deck chair	office	swimming pool
diving board	pay phone	swimming suit

B. Study these words and their meanings. Then look for examples of these objects and activities in the picture.

cactus   (n) a plant that lives in hot, dry places
cowboy hat   (n) a cloth hat with a wide brim
desert   (n) a dry, sandy area of land
to dive   (v) to jump headfirst into water
mule   (n) an animal that is half-horse and half-donkey
prospector   (n) someone who looks for gold or other minerals
scuba diver   (n) someone who swims underwater wearing special breathing equipment
to splash   (v) to make water fly about
to sunbathe   (v) to lie in the sun
suntan   (n) skin darkened by the sun
vulture   (n) a large bird that eats dead animals

C. Here are some other words you can use to talk about a motel. Study these words and their meanings.

air-conditioned   (adj) cooled by a special machine
to check in   (v) to give your name and get your room key
to check out   (v) to pay and return your key
double room   (n) a room for two people
guest   (n) someone who is staying at a motel
laundromat   (n) a place where people can pay to use washing machines and dryers
reservation   (n) an arrangement to use something (such as a motel room) at a certain time
to reserve   (v) to make a reservation
single room   (n) a room for one person
suite   (n) two or more connecting rooms
vacancy   (n) an empty space

Now complete these sentences with words from List C. Change the form of a word if necessary.

1. Let's _____ to the motel and then go swimming.

2. You must _____ before noon or pay for another night.

3. A room for two people is a _____ room.

4. Dennis _____ a room at the hotel in Danville.

5. It's so hot! Is your apartment _____ ?

Understanding the Picture

1. What is the name of this motel?

2. In what part of the United States is this motel located?

3. Does this motel have any empty rooms today?

4. Does this motel have a parking lot?

5. Is there anyplace to eat at this motel?

6. Which of these things can guests do at this motel?

a. watch television	e. rent a car
b. go swimming	f. wash clothes
c. wash dishes	g. buy a meal
d. sleep	h. make a phone call

7. Which of these animals do you see in the picture?

a. cat
b. dog
c. mule
d. duck
e. vulture
f. owl
g. cow
h. fish

8. There are many guests at this motel. Which of these things are they doing?

a. getting ice
b. swimming
c. air-conditioning
d. sunbathing
e. parking
f. looking for a room
g. diving
h. eating

What Do You See?

Study this part of the picture. Then answer the questions.

1. What is happening in the swimming pool?

2. What is the man in the pink shirt doing?

3. What is happening by the ice machine?

4. What is happening on the balcony?

5. What is the dog doing?

What Are They Saying?

The woman in the yellow skirt is talking to the employee at the front desk. Practice their conversation with a partner.

EMPLOYEE: Hi. May I help you?

WOMAN: Yes. I need a single room, please.

EMPLOYEE: Do you have a reservation?

WOMAN: No, I don't.

EMPLOYEE: Okay. What's your name?

WOMAN: Carmen Dole. D-O-L-E.

EMPLOYEE: How many nights will you be staying?

WOMAN: Just one.

EMPLOYEE: That will be forty-five dollars.

WOMAN: May I write a check?

EMPLOYEE: Yes, if I can see your driver's license.

WOMAN: Sure. *(pause)* Here you go.

EMPLOYEE: Thank you. Here's your room key. You're upstairs in room 12.

WOMAN: Okay. Thank you very much.

Now work with your partner to change the conversation so that

- The woman will be staying for two nights.
- The room costs forty dollars a night.
- The woman will pay for the room with a credit card.
- The employee needs to see the credit card now.
- The woman is in room 4.

Practice your new conversation together.

What Will Happen Next?

Answer these questions in small groups. Then compare your answers with those of the other groups.

1. What will happen to the girl in the pink bikini?

2. What will happen to the man with the cowboy hat?

3. What will the children by the ice machine do next?

What Would You Say?

Act out this situation with a partner. Take turns playing parts A and B.

A. You are checking into a motel. You have a reservation for a double room for three nights. You will use a credit card to pay for your room. You ask for a nonsmoking room on the second floor.

B. You are an employee at the front desk of a motel. You know that a double room costs seventy-five dollars a night. All the nonsmoking rooms are on the first floor.

What Do You See?

Study this part of the picture. Then answer the questions.

1. Who are the people with the white cowboy hats?

2. What is on the restaurant tables?

3. What is the girl in the striped shorts doing?

4. What are the people in the deck chairs doing?

5. What are the people in the pool doing?

What Are They Saying?

The waitress is talking to the couple at the table. Practice their conversation in groups of three.

WAITRESS: Are you ready to order?

WOMAN: Yes. I'll have the Desert Salad.

WAITRESS: What kind of dressing do you want? We have French, Italian, and blue cheese.

WOMAN: I'll have Italian, please.

WAITRESS: Would you like anything to drink?

WOMAN: Do you have iced tea?

WAITRESS: Yes.

WOMAN: I'll have that.

WAITRESS: And what about you, sir?

MAN: I'll have the Big Sands Burger and iced tea.

WAITRESS: Do you want french fries with your burger?

MAN: Yes, please.

WAITRESS: Okay. I'll bring your drinks out in just a minute.

Now work with your group to change the conversation so that

- The woman wants to have the taco platter.
- The waitress asks if she wants chicken tacos or beef tacos.
- The man wants to have the burrito special.
- The waitress asks if he wants refried beans.

Practice your new conversation together.

What Will Happen Next?

Answer these questions in small groups. Then compare your answers with those of the other groups.

1. What will the girl in the red swimming suit do next?

2. What will the girl in the yellow deck chair do next?

3. What will happen to the prospector and his mule?

What Would You Say?

Act out this situation in groups of three. Take turns playing parts A, B, and C.

A. You are a waiter at the Pizza Palace. You are taking a couple's order. You ask if they want salads with their pizza.

B. You and your boyfriend are ordering a meal at the Pizza Palace. You ask the waiter how big the small, medium, and large pizzas are. You tell the waiter what you want to drink.

C. You and your girlfriend are ordering a meal at the Pizza Palace. You tell the waiter what kind of pizza you want and what you want to drink.

Let's Practice

The Last Chance Motel has sixty rooms for guests.
This line graph shows how many of the rooms were
occupied (rented by guests) during January and May.

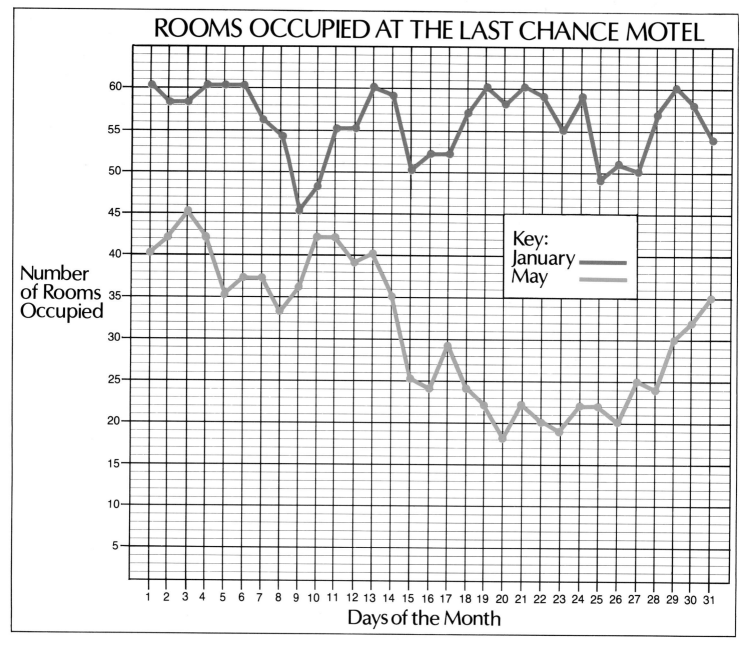

Now work with a partner to answer these questions.

1. How many rooms were occupied on January 4?

2. How many rooms were occupied on May 29?

3. How many rooms were occupied on January 11?

4. Were more rooms occupied on January 15 or on May 15?

5. Were more rooms occupied on January 1 or on May 1?

6. Were more rooms occupied on May 22 or on May 31?

7. On which day(s) in January were the most rooms occupied?

8. On which day(s) in May were the most rooms occupied?

9. On which day(s) in May were the fewest rooms occupied?

10. If every room was occupied by one guest, how many guests stayed at the motel on January 9?

11. If every room was occupied by two guests, how many guests stayed at the motel on May 5?

12. Were more rooms occupied in January or in May?

Let's Learn More

Read these paragraphs about U.S. motels and hotels.

Because Americans travel so often for business and for fun, there are more than 44,000 hotels and motels in the United States. These hotels and motels have more than three million rooms available for guests. In fact, some cities have enough hotel and motel rooms to hold all the **residents** of a large town. For example, New York City and Orlando, Florida, each have around 70,000 rooms.

A motel is a special kind of hotel. Its name comes from the words *motor* and *hotel.* Many motels are located on or near major highways, and they usually provide a free place for guests to park their cars. The first U.S. motels were built in the late 1920s, when the car became a popular way to travel. The number of U.S. motels grew quickly after World War II, as more highways were built and more Americans owned cars. Today, most motels are part of nationwide **chains.**

Unlike motels, most hotels are located in the middle of a city or town. They usually offer guests many **services.** Some hotels have free parking, but many others do not. Most hotels have one or more restaurants in the building.

Traditionally, the price of a room at an American hotel or motel does not include any meals. However, some chains are starting to offer guests a free breakfast with the price of a room. Another recent **trend** is hotels and motels that offer suites instead of regular rooms. Swimming pools are a popular **attraction** offered by most American hotels and motels.

Vocabulary Check

Study these words and their meanings.

attraction   (n) something that makes people want to come nearer; something that interests people
chain   (n) a group of businesses that are owned by the same company and have the same name
resident   (n) someone who lives in a place
service   (n) something that helps people or is useful
trend   (n) a movement; a direction of development

Now find words in the reading that have these meanings.

1. without payment

2. breakfasts, lunches, and dinners

3. people who live in a place

4. people who are staying in a hotel or motel

5. things that are helpful or useful

Comprehension Check

Match the two parts of each sentence.

1. At most U.S. hotels and motels, the price of a room

2. The word *motel* comes from

3. Most U.S. hotels and motels have

4. Most U.S. motels offer

5. Most U.S. hotels

6. Most U.S. motels are part of

a. have at least one restaurant.

b. large nationwide chains.

c. the words *motor* and *hotel.*

d. doesn't include breakfast.

e. free parking to their guests.

f. swimming pools.

Extension Activity

In groups of four, plan a new hotel or motel for your city or town. Where will it be located? Why? Will it be a hotel or a motel? How many rooms will it have? Will it have a restaurant? a swimming pool? a parking lot? What other services will it have? Give your hotel or motel a name.

Billboards (big signs by a highway) are often used to tell travelers about nearby hotels and motels. With your group, make a billboard on poster board or a big piece of paper to advertise your hotel or motel.

Display all the billboards in your classroom. Walk around and look at the billboards. If you were a traveler looking for a place to spend the night, which hotel or motel would you choose? Let each student vote for the hotel or motel he would go to. Which hotel or motel is the winner?

Talk about the billboards and the hotels/motels. Why did the billboard for the winning hotel or motel attract so many people? What makes a good billboard? What makes a good motel or hotel?

Unit Four
Just for Fun

Having fun is an important part of life in the United States. In good weather, the country's parks and beaches are full of people relaxing and enjoying nature. Playgrounds and amusement parks provide other exciting outdoor activities. Many Americans go to concerts, plays, and movies during their free time. And, of course, Americans enjoy watching and participating in many different sports.

Chapter 15: A High School Sports Meet shows American high school students competing in several sports. In this chapter, you will study and talk about popular sports in the United States. You will also learn and practice the language Americans use when they're watching and playing a variety of sports.

Chapter 16: At the Park and **Chapter 17: At the Beach** show us two places Americans go to relax outside. In these chapters, you will talk about a variety of outdoor sports and activities and practice using information from maps and signs.

Chapter 18: Winter Sports and Activities shows what Americans do for fun when the weather is cold and/or snowy. Sledding, ice-skating, and skiing are some of the popular activities you will talk about in this chapter.

Chapter 19: At an Outdoor Concert provides a chance to "see" an American rock concert—and to "hear" what Americans have to say about their rock stars. You will also practice buying souvenirs.

Chapter 20: At an Amusement Park ends the unit with the excitement of an American amusement park. You will practice buying tickets and following a map to find your favorite rides.

Chapter 15
A High School Sports Meet

Warm-Up

❑ Do you enjoy playing any sports?
If so, which ones?

❑ Do you enjoy watching any sports?
If so, which ones?

Words to Know

A. Here are the names of some things you can find at a sports meet. Look for them in the picture.

basketball	hurdle	spectator
cheerleader	mascot	starting pistol
coach	player	track
football	referee	uniform
helmet	scoreboard	volleyball

B. Here are some other words you can use to talk about sports. Study these words and their meanings.

athlete (n) someone who is good at sports
to be tied (v) to have the same score
to compete (v) to be in a contest or race
high jump (n) a field event in which competitors jump over a crossbar
to lead (v) to be winning; to be ahead
long jump (n) a field event in which competitors jump as far as they can
to make a touchdown (v) to score in football by moving the ball across the other team's goal line
meet (n) a competition
to participate (v) to take part; to be involved
race (n) a track event in which runners compete to run a certain distance in the shortest time
score (n) the number of points made in a game
to score (v) to gain points in a game

to shoot (v) to try to score in basketball by throwing the ball toward the basket
shot put (n) a field event in which competitors throw a heavy metal ball as far as they can
to tackle (v) to stop a football player who has the ball by throwing him to the ground
track and field (adj) having to do with a group of sporting events that take place on a running track and on the grassy field inside the track

C. Here are more words you can use to talk about the objects and activities in the picture.

bulldog	locker room	stopwatch
camera	photographer	to stuff
to cheer	press box	(a basketball)
dizzy	reporter	ticket booth
field house	snack bar	tiger
locker	to spill	to trip

Now complete these sentences with words from List B. Change the form of a word if necessary.

1. —What's the _____ in the baseball game?
   —It's four to three. The Jets are _____ .

2. One way to score in football is to make a _____ .

3. The _____ and the _____ are two track and field events.

Understanding the Picture

1. What teams are playing in this sports meet?

2. Which team is leading in the basketball game?

3. Which team is leading in the football game?

4. Which of these sports do you see in the picture?

   a. basketball   e. volleyball
   b. tennis   f. football
   c. golf   g. baseball
   d. track and field   h. wrestling

5. Find someone in the picture who is doing each of these things.

a. taking pictures
b. selling tickets
c. cheering
d. falling down
e. buying a snack
f. waiting in line
g. starting a race
h. talking about a game

6. Which of these kinds of sports equipment do you see in the picture?

a. volleyball net
b. football helmet
c. basketball hoop
d. shoulder pads
e. goalpost
f. baseball bat
g. hurdle
h. golf club

What other kinds of sports equipment do you see in the picture?

What Do You See?

Study this part of the picture. Then answer the questions.

1. What are the animals on the field?

2. What happened to the high jumper?

3. What is happening in the field house?

4. What are the girls on the track doing?

5. What is happening to the shot-putter?

What Are They Saying?

Two of the basketball spectators are talking about the game. Practice their conversation with a partner.

SPECTATOR 1: Did you see that? O'Reilly stuffed it again!

SPECTATOR 2: He's going to have another great game today!

SPECTATOR 1: No kidding! Did you see the game last week against the Giants?

SPECTATOR 2: Yes! O'Reilly scored thirty points!

SPECTATOR 1: It's hard to believe he's only a sophomore.

SPECTATOR 2: Yeah. He'll be on the team for two more years!

SPECTATOR 1: I wonder where he'll go to college.

SPECTATOR 2: I don't know. I'm sure he'll get a great basketball scholarship.

SPECTATOR 1: Well, I'm glad O'Reilly's on our team for now.

SPECTATOR 2: Me, too. I'm happy I'm not cheering for the Bulldogs today!

Now work with your partner to change the conversation so that

- O'Reilly scored thirty-five points last week against the Lions.
- O'Reilly is a senior.
- The Tigers will miss him next year.
- O'Reilly is going to Wright University on a basketball scholarship.

Practice your new conversation together.

What Will Happen Next?

Answer these questions in small groups. Then compare your answers with those of the other groups.

1. What is the girl with the number 2 on her back going to do?

2. What will the high jumper do next?

3. Which team will win the basketball game?

What Would You Say?

Act out this situation with a partner. Take turns playing parts A and B.

A. You are a spectator at a football game. One of the players on your team makes a touchdown. You ask your friend who the player is.

B. You are a spectator at a football game. You know all about the players on your team. You tell your friend about this player. He works hard and always plays well.

What Do You See?

Study this part of the picture. Then answer the questions.

1. What is the player with the football doing?

2. What are the referees doing?

3. What special equipment are the football players wearing?

4. What is happening in the locker room?

5. What is the man in the press box doing?

What Are They Saying?

The Tigers' volleyball coach is talking to her team in the locker room. Practice their conversation in groups of three.

COACH: Now girls, I'm not angry that we lost the game. The Bulldogs are a good team. I'm just upset because I don't think you played your best.

PLAYER 1: May I say something, Mrs. Fujimoto?

COACH: Of course, Kelley.

PLAYER 1: It doesn't matter how well we play. The Bulldogs always beat us.

PLAYER 2: Yeah. We just don't try anymore.

COACH: I'm surprised at you girls. Good athletes always try!

PLAYER 2: Even if you know you're going to lose?

COACH: Of course. Besides, you can beat those Bulldogs. You have me for a coach now!

Now work with your group to change the conversation so that

- The players tell the coach that they are tired today. They all had exams this morning.
- The coach asks why they didn't tell her about the exams before.
- They didn't think she would care.
- The coach cares a lot about her players. They should tell her when they have problems. Maybe she can help.

Practice your new conversation together.

What Will Happen Next?

Answer these questions in small groups. Then compare your answers with those of the other groups.

1. What will happen to the football player who is standing outside the locker room?

2. What will the cheerleaders do next?

3. What will the man in the press box do when the game is over?

What Would You Say?

Act out this situation in groups of three. Take turns playing parts A, B, and C.

A. You are a basketball coach talking to your team at halftime. Your team is leading by two points. You want your players to work harder.

B. You are a basketball player on A's team. You tell the coach you don't have to work hard to beat the Eagles.

C. You are a player on A's team. You agree with the coach. The Eagles could win if your team doesn't work harder.

Let's Practice

Look at this sports schedule for Riverton High School.
Then work with a partner to answer the questions.

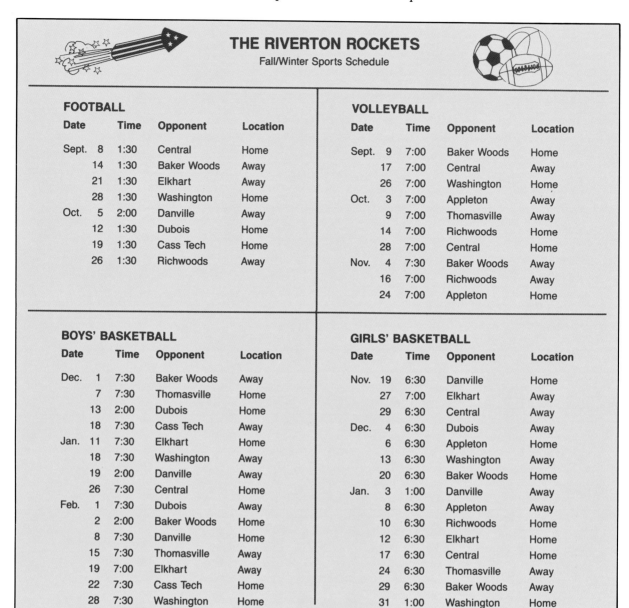

THE RIVERTON ROCKETS
Fall/Winter Sports Schedule

FOOTBALL

Date	Time	Opponent	Location
Sept. 8	1:30	Central	Home
14	1:30	Baker Woods	Away
21	1:30	Elkhart	Away
28	1:30	Washington	Home
Oct. 5	2:00	Danville	Away
12	1:30	Dubois	Home
19	1:30	Cass Tech	Home
26	1:30	Richwoods	Away

VOLLEYBALL

Date	Time	Opponent	Location
Sept. 9	7:00	Baker Woods	Home
17	7:00	Central	Away
26	7:00	Washington	Home
Oct. 3	7:00	Appleton	Away
9	7:00	Thomasville	Away
14	7:00	Richwoods	Home
28	7:00	Central	Home
Nov. 4	7:30	Baker Woods	Away
16	7:00	Richwoods	Away
24	7:00	Appleton	Home

BOYS' BASKETBALL

Date	Time	Opponent	Location
Dec. 1	7:30	Baker Woods	Away
7	7:30	Thomasville	Home
13	2:00	Dubois	Home
18	7:30	Cass Tech	Away
Jan. 11	7:30	Elkhart	Home
18	7:30	Washington	Away
19	2:00	Danville	Away
26	7:30	Central	Home
Feb. 1	7:30	Dubois	Away
2	2:00	Baker Woods	Home
8	7:30	Danville	Home
15	7:30	Thomasville	Away
19	7:00	Elkhart	Away
22	7:30	Cass Tech	Home
28	7:30	Washington	Home

GIRLS' BASKETBALL

Date	Time	Opponent	Location
Nov. 19	6:30	Danville	Home
27	7:00	Elkhart	Away
29	6:30	Central	Away
Dec. 4	6:30	Dubois	Away
6	6:30	Appleton	Home
13	6:30	Washington	Away
20	6:30	Baker Woods	Home
Jan. 3	1:00	Danville	Away
8	6:30	Appleton	Away
10	6:30	Richwoods	Home
12	6:30	Elkhart	Home
17	6:30	Central	Home
24	6:30	Thomasville	Away
29	6:30	Baker Woods	Away
31	1:00	Washington	Home

Understanding the Schedule

1. Which sports are included on this schedule?

2. What time of year are these sports played?

3. Which teams are playing in September?

4. Which teams are playing in January?

5. Which team plays the first game of the school year?

Following the Schedule

1. How many times does the girls' basketball team play Baker Woods?

2. How many times does the boys' basketball team play Elkhart?

3. How many schools does the football team play?

Using the Schedule

1. You want to see all of the volleyball team's home games this year. What days will those games be?

2. You don't want to miss the football game against Cass Tech. When is it?

3. You want to go to a sporting event on November 24. What game(s) can you see?

4. You want to go to a sporting event on December 13. What game(s) can you see?

Let's Learn More

Read these paragraphs about sports in the United States.

Sports play a big part in the lives of many Americans. Students of all ages must take physical education classes, in which they learn to play many sports. Students can also play on school sports teams that compete with teams from other schools. Many Americans believe that sports teach students important things like **teamwork** and **sportsmanship.** Americans also see sports as an important form of exercise.

Many Americans enjoy watching sports as much as participating in them. High school and college sporting events often **attract** many spectators. Professional sporting events also attract large **crowds.** In addition, millions of Americans watch college and professional sporting events on television.

The high **value** placed on athletes in the United States is clear from their **salaries.** For example, the lowest salary for a professional baseball player is about $100,000. Most professional basketball players earn between $100,000 and three million dollars a year—but most U.S. college professors earn just $20,000 to $80,000 a year.

The three most popular sports in the United States are American football, baseball, and basketball. Other common sports include track-and-field events, volleyball, wrestling, tennis, swimming, soccer (European football), and golf.

Vocabulary Check

Study these words and their meanings.

to attract   (v) to make someone want to come nearer
crowd   (n) a big group of people
salary   (n) regular pay for a job
sportsmanship   (n) a spirit of honesty and fairness in playing a game; an ability to win and lose gracefully
teamwork   (n) the ability to work well with a group of people
value   (n) importance; worth

Now find words in the reading that have these meanings.

1. big groups of people

2. taking part

3. money people get for doing their jobs

4. people who are good at sports

5. people who are watching something

Comprehension Check

Match the two parts of each sentence.

1. Professional basketball players usually earn

2. The most popular sports in the United States are

3. Sports are an important

4. Students learn to play many sports in their

5. Many Americans think sports teach students about

a. form of exercise.

b. physical education classes.

c. $100,000 to $3,000,000 a year.

d. sportsmanship and teamwork.

e. baseball, basketball, and American football.

Extension Activity

Choose a sport that you know well—for example, one that is popular in your native country but not in the United States. Prepare a short talk that explains how to play this sport. Tell where it is played, how many players are needed, what equipment is used, and so forth. Briefly explain the rules and the object of the sport. Give your talk in front of the class. If possible, bring in some pictures of the sport or examples of the equipment. Answer any questions your classmates have about the sport. (You can work individually, in pairs, or in small groups to prepare and give your talks.)

Chapter 16
At the Park

Warm-Up

❑ Why do people go to parks?   ❑ What do you like to do at a park?

Words to Know

A. Here are the names of some things you can find at a park. Look for them in the picture.

balloon	helmet	pond
bicycle	kite	roller skates
bush	lawn chair	skateboard
chin-up bar	leaf	snack bar
drinking fountain	paddleboat	statue
flower	park bench	tennis racket
Frisbee	path	toy sailboat
grass	picnic table	tree

B. Many activities take place at a park. Look for examples of these activities in the picture.

to climb a tree	to rake
to crash into something	to read
to feed the birds	to ride a bicycle
to have a picnic	to ride a skateboard
to jog	to roller-skate
to play an instrument	to wait in line
to play Frisbee	to walk a dog

C. Study these words and their meanings. Then look for examples of these objects and activities in the picture.

band   (n) a group of people playing musical instruments

banjo   (n) a musical instrument with a round body, a long neck, and four or five strings

boom box   (n) a portable stereo radio, cassette, or CD player

fin   (n) a wing-like body part of a fish or other water animal

free   (adj) not costing any money

jazz   (n) a kind of music with special rhythms that developed from blues music

leash   (n) a long, strong cord that attaches to an animal's collar

mounted police officer   (n) a police officer who rides a horse around the area he watches

to rent   (v) to pay money to use something for a certain amount of time

to sink   (v) to go underwater

to squirt   (v) to make water or some other liquid come out of an opening suddenly and quickly

training wheels   (n) two small wheels that help hold a bicycle up while a person is learning to ride

Now complete these sentences with words from Lists B and C. Change the form of a word if necessary.

1. Jack is _____ leaves outside.

2. Kim plays the trumpet in our school _____ .

3. —Roy, will you please _____ the dog?
   —Okay. Do you know where his _____ is?

4. It's a beautiful day. Let's _____ for lunch.

Understanding the Picture

1. Find someone in the picture who is doing each of these things.

   a. having a picnic   e. listening to a story
   b. squirting water   f. walking a dog
   c. flying a kite   g. picking flowers
   d. climbing a tree   h. waiting in line

2. Which of these activities are free at this park?

   a. listening to the band concert
   b. getting something at the snack bar
   c. riding in a paddleboat
   d. going to the zoo
   e. jogging on a path

3. Which of these kinds of sporting equipment do you see at this park?

a. baseball bat   f. bicycle helmet
b. tennis racket   g. volleyball net
c. Frisbee   h. bowling pins
d. football   i. roller skates
e. skateboard   j. fishing rod

What other kinds of sporting equipment do you see in the picture?

4. Most of the people at this park are here to have fun. However, some of them are working.
Which of these jobs do you see in the picture?

a. selling food   e. selling balloons
b. buying food   f. feeding the birds
c. playing a musical   g. raking leaves
   instrument   h. riding a bicycle
d. riding a horse

What Do You See?

Study this part of the picture.
Then answer the questions.

1. What is the giraffe doing?

2. What is happening in the pond?

3. What are the children doing?

4. How much do the balloons cost?

5. What are the men in the striped shirts doing?

What Are They Saying?

The man in the blue shirt and brown slacks is talking to his son. Practice their conversation with a partner.

BOY: Hey, Dad! Look at those neat balloons! Can I have one?

MAN: I don't think you need a balloon, Stuart.

BOY: Please, Dad? I really like the blue one with the dolphin on it.

MAN: We just bought you that hat with the moose antlers, Stuart. I'm not buying anything else today.

BOY: But the balloons are only a dollar fifty!

MAN: I said no, Stuart. Now, do you want to go to the zoo or stay out here and listen to the band?

BOY: Let's go to the zoo! I don't want to listen to that yucky music.

MAN: Oh, Stuart. Jazz music isn't yucky. Your mother and I really enjoy it.

BOY: Come on, let's go look at the bears.

Now work with your partner to change the conversation so that

- Stuart likes the purple balloon with the bear on it.
- Stuart's dad tells him he can buy a balloon with his own money.
- Stuart already spent all of his money.
- Stuart's dad wants to listen to the band before they go to the zoo.
- Stuart says he will listen to the music for a few minutes.

Practice your new conversation together.

What Will Happen Next?

Answer these questions in small groups. Then compare your answers with those of the other groups.

1. What will happen to the children who are in the tree?

2. What will happen to the children who are flying kites?

3. What will the band members do after their concert?

What Would You Say?

Act out this situation with a partner. Take turns playing parts A and B.

A. You and your friend are deciding what to do at a big park. You want to buy some food at the snack bar, then rent a paddleboat and go out on the pond.

B. You and your friend are deciding what to do at a big park. You want to go to the zoo. Then you want to ride your bicycle on the paths and rent a paddleboat. You don't want to waste your time eating.

What Do You See?

Study this part of the picture. Then answer the questions.

1. What is the woman in the blue dress doing by the statue?

2. What happened to the boy bicycle rider?

3. What is the big dog by the picnic table doing?

4. What is the boy on the skateboard carrying?

5. What is the squirrel doing?

What Are They Saying?

The boy who fell off his bicycle is talking to the girl bicycle rider. Practice their conversation with a partner.

BOY: Hey, watch it! You pushed me off the path.

GIRL: I'm sorry. I didn't mean to get in your way.

BOY: Maybe you should practice riding someplace that's not so busy.

GIRL: Maybe so. Oh, look! Your wheel is bent!

BOY: That's okay. I think my uncle can fix it.

GIRL: I hope so. I'm really sorry.

BOY: Don't worry. It was an accident. But this is a dangerous place for you to ride. Someone could crash into you!

GIRL: You're right. Everyone moves so quickly here!

BOY: Well, I can't move quickly now. I'll have to walk home with my bike.

GIRL: Is it okay if I walk a little way with you? I walk much better than I ride!

Now work with your partner to change the conversation so that

- The girl says that the boy on the skateboard scared her.
- The boy thinks he can fix his bicycle wheel.
- The girl wants to buy him a new wheel if he can't fix it.
- The girl is going to pick up the trash can. Then she'll walk home with her bike, too.

Practice your new conversation together.

What Will Happen Next?

Answer these questions in small groups. Then compare your answers with those of the other groups.

1. What will happen to the big dog by the picnic table?
2. What will happen to the little dog by the statue?
3. What will the girl on the roller skates do next?

What Would You Say?

Act out this situation with a partner. Take turns playing parts A and B.

A. You are roller-skating in the park. A girl on a skateboard crashes into you. You fall down and cut your knee. You also spill your soda.

B. You are riding a skateboard in the park. You are hurrying to meet your brother. You accidentally crash into someone who is roller-skating. You stop to see if that skater is okay.

Let's Practice

Look at this map of Willow Tree Park. Then work with a partner to answer the questions.

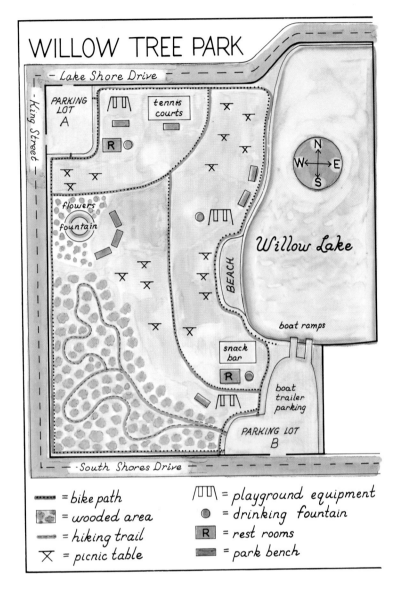

WILLOW TREE PARK

Lake Shore Drive

King Street

PARKING LOT A

tennis courts

R

flowers
fountain

Willow Lake

BEACH

boat ramps

snack bar

R

boat trailer parking

PARKING LOT B

South Shores Drive

= *bike path*
= *wooded area*
= *hiking trail*
= *picnic table*
= *playground equipment*
= *drinking fountain*
R = *rest rooms*
= *park bench*

Understanding the Map

Use the map to answer these questions about Willow Tree Park.

1. How many parking lots are there at Willow Tree Park?

2. Is there a swimming pool at Willow Tree Park?

3. How many picnic tables are there at Willow Tree Park?

4. Is there a fountain at Willow Tree Park?

5. Are there any rest rooms at Willow Tree Park?

Following Directions

We use the words **north, south, east,** and **west** to talk about directions. The map shows these directions with arrows:

Complete these sentences about Willow Tree Park with the words **north, south, east,** and **west.**

Example: The lake is __east__ of the tennis courts.

1. The hiking trails are _____ of the fountain.

2. The snack bar is _____ of the boat ramps.

3. Parking Lot A is _____ of the fountain.

4. The lake is on the _____ side of the park.

5. The beach is _____ of the snack bar.

Giving Directions

Tell your friend where to find you at Willow Tree Park. Use the words **left, right, north, south, east,** and **west.**

Example: Your friend will park his car in Parking Lot B. You will be at a picnic table by the beach.

Walk north on the bike path out of Parking Lot B.

You will see some playground equipment on your

left. Keep walking until you see the snack bar and

the beach. I will be at the first table west of the

beach.

1. Your friend will get off the bus at the corner of King Street and South Shores Drive. You will be at the boat ramps.

2. Your friend will park her car in Parking Lot A. You will be at the tennis courts.

3. Your friend will ride his bike west on Lake Shore Drive to the park. You will be at the fountain.

Let's Learn More

Read these paragraphs about public parks in the United States.

Most cities and towns in the United States have one or more public parks. Some parks are small, while others cover several **acres** of land. Most parks have a lot of grassy land, which provides space for people to play baseball or other games, have picnics, or simply lie on a blanket and read. Some parks also have **wooded** areas with trails for hiking.

Most parks have picnic tables, park benches, drinking fountains, paths for jogging or bicycling, and playground equipment such as swings, slides, and **monkey bars.** Some parks have beautiful flowers, statues, and fountains. A few large parks have special **facilities** such as swimming pools, zoos, snack bars, and lakes or ponds for boating. People usually must pay to use these special facilities, but the other parts of a public park are free for anyone to use. Local governments use tax money to buy and repair park equipment and to pay for park programs.

Most Americans enjoy going to parks to relax or exercise outdoors. Parks are especially important to people who live in big cities, because they may not have any other place to spend time outdoors. If there were no public parks, many children growing up in cities would have nowhere to play outside except in the streets.

Vocabulary Check

Study these words and their meanings.

acre   (n) a unit of area; about 4,000 square meters
facility   (n) a place for doing a certain activity
monkey bars   (n) wooden or metal bars for children to climb, swing, and hang on
wooded   (adj) full of trees

Now choose the best word to complete each sentence.

1. This apartment building doesn't have any _____ for washing clothes. (monkey bars, facilities)

2. I'm thirsty. Does this park have a _____ ? (fountain, drinking fountain)

3. —Are there any trees in this park?
   —Yes. There's a big _____ area behind the zoo. (wooded, grassy)

4. My bicycle is broken. Can you _____ it? (buy, repair)

Comprehension Check

Choose the correct answers for each question. Each question may have one, two, three, or four correct answers.

1. Which of these things can you find at most parks?

   a. playground equipment   c. grass
   b. picnic tables   d. paths

2. Which of these things can you do at a park?

   a. exercise   c. lie on a blanket and read
   b. have a picnic   d. wash your clothes

3. Which of these park facilities do people usually have to pay to use?

   a. a slide   c. a park bench
   b. a swimming pool   d. a hiking trail

Extension Activity

With a partner, talk about the parks in your community. Choose one park that you both know well. Make a list of three things you and your partner like about that park. Then make a list of three things you don't like about that park.

Talk about ways to improve the park. What could the city do? What could the people who use the park do?

With your partner, write a letter to the editor of your community newspaper. Tell what you like about the park and what you don't like about it. Then tell what you think people should do to improve the park.

Exchange letters with another pair of students. Read your classmates' letter. Tell them if you see any mistakes or if you can't understand any parts of the letter. Listen to what they say about your letter. Then write a final copy of your letter. Mail it to the newspaper office and watch to see it in the paper!

Chapter 17

At the Beach

Warm-Up

❏ Why do people go to a beach?   ❏ What do you like to do at the beach?

Words to Know

A.   Here are the names of some things you can find at a beach. Look for them in the picture.

barbecue grill	fly (insect)	rowboat
beach ball	food stand	sailboat
beach towel	lifeguard	sand
bikini	life preserver	sand castle
cooler	motor boat	sunscreen
crab	picnic table	surfboard
fishing rod	pier	swimsuit

B.   Many activities take place at a beach. Look for examples of these activities in the picture.

to fish	to snorkel	to surf
to float	to splash	to swim
to grill	to sunbathe	

C.   Here are more words you can use to talk about the beach. Study these words and their meanings. Then look for examples of these objects and activities in the picture.

barbecue   (n) a meal that is cooked outdoors over a fire and then eaten outdoors; also called a cookout

boardwalk   (n) a path or sidewalk made of wooden boards

on duty   (adj) on the job; working

shark   (n) a large, dangerous fish that lives in the ocean

snorkeling   (n) swimming underwater while wearing a breathing tube called a snorkel. The top of the snorkel stays above the water, in the air.

sunburn   (n) burning of the skin by the rays of the sun

suntan   (n) darkening of the skin by the rays of the sun

to tangle   (v) to twist together and get mixed up

whistle   (n) a small instrument that makes a loud, sharp sound when a person blows it

Now complete these sentences with words from List C. Change the form of a word if necessary.

1.   Marti stayed out in the sun too long. Now she has a painful _____ .

2.   Winnie and Jack like to cook outside when it's warm. They often have _____ in their back yard.

3.   Many people enjoy _____ because they can watch the fish and other life underwater.

4.   It's dangerous to go swimming alone when there's no lifeguard _____ .

5.   Many Americans feel more attractive when they have a _____ .

Understanding the Picture

1.   Which of these things did someone bring to this beach today?

a. beach towel	f. sunglasses
b. picnic table	g. sand castle
c. surfboard	h. fishing rod
d. radio	i. bucket
e. crab	j. boardwalk

2.   Which of these vehicles do you see in the picture?

a. car	e. rowboat
b. tow truck	f. sailboat
c. motor boat	g. helicopter
d. tractor	h. motorcycle

What other vehicle(s) do you see in the picture?

3. Find someone in the picture who is doing each
of these things.

a. putting on sunscreen
b. grilling hamburgers
c. buying food
d. calling for help
e. dancing to music
f. blowing a whistle

What Do You See?

Study this part of the picture. Then answer the questions.

1. What are the two people on the boardwalk doing?

2. What is the lifeguard doing?

3. What is happening at the picnic table?

4. What did the man with the red hat bring to the beach?

5. What are the young people with the buckets doing?

What Are They Saying?

The young man lying on the beach towel is talking to the young woman in the purple bikini. Practice their conversation with a partner.

MAN: Hey, Jill! Try not to get that sunscreen in my hair.

WOMAN: Sorry, Carlos. I was just putting it on your shoulders.

MAN: Do you think you're putting enough on?

WOMAN: I think so, honey.

MAN: That was a joke! It feels like you're putting on too much!

WOMAN: I have to cover your skin. You don't want to get a sunburn, do you?

MAN: No, but I do like to have a nice suntan.

WOMAN: I know. I do, too. But I read another magazine article about skin cancer yesterday. It's really dangerous to be out in the sun without sunscreen.

MAN: Okay, okay. But I think I'm wearing enough now. Why don't you lie down so I can put some on your back?

Now work with your partner to change the conversation so that

- Jill was putting sunscreen on Carlos's neck.
- Jill doesn't think she's putting enough on. She wants to put more on his legs.
- Carlos doesn't think he will get a sunburn. His skin never burns.
- Jill saw a TV show about skin cancer last week.
- Carlos saw the same TV show.

Practice your new conversation together.

What Will Happen Next?

Answer these questions in small groups. Then compare your answers with those of the other groups.

1. What will the people at the picnic table do next?

2. What will the woman in the purple bikini do next?

3. What will happen to the young people with the buckets?

What Would You Say?

Act out this situation in groups of three. Take turns playing parts A, B, and C.

A. You are at the beach with two friends. You forgot to bring your sunscreen. Your skin burns easily, so you ask your friends if they have any sunscreen.

B. You are at the beach with two friends. You never use sunscreen, because you like to have a great tan.

C. You are at the beach with two friends. Your mother always tells you to use sunscreen, so you won't get skin cancer. You have sunscreen with you today.

What Do You See?

Study this part of the picture. Then answer the questions.

1. What are the children doing?

2. What are the two women doing by the water?

3. What is happening in the water?

4. What is the girl in the pink T-shirt doing?

5. Why does the man on the striped beach towel look unhappy?

What Are They Saying?

The two women by the water are talking to each other. Practice their conversation with a partner.

WOMAN 1: I wonder if the water is cold.

WOMAN 2: I hope not! It was pretty warm last weekend.

WOMAN 1: It's not too bad. What do you think?

WOMAN 2: It feels a little chilly to me.

WOMAN 1: Wait a minute. Who's that in the water?

WOMAN 2: It looks like Fred Hawkins.

WOMAN 1: Oh, no. I don't want to see him.

WOMAN 2: He wants to see you! He's waving at us.

WOMAN 1: I'm not going to wave back. There are too many people in the water here. Let's look for a better place to swim.

WOMAN 2: Good idea. Let's walk toward the pier. I don't see many people in the water over there.

Now work with your partner to change the conversation so that

- The water was pretty cold last weekend.
- Woman 2 thinks the water feels fine.
- The man in the water is Woman 1's neighbor, Jason.
- Woman 1 thinks the water looks dirty here.
- Woman 2 thinks the water looks cleaner by the pier.

Practice your new conversation together.

What Will Happen Next?

Answer these questions in small groups. Then compare your answers with those of the other groups.

1. What will the children do next?

2. What will the man on the striped beach towel do next?

3. What will happen to the three boys playing in the water?

What Would You Say?

Act out this situation with a partner. Take turns playing parts A and B.

A. You and your friend are looking for a place to put your towels at the beach. You see a good place by the lifeguard's chair. You want to put your towel down and get in the water.

B. You and your friend are looking for a place to put your towels at the beach. You don't want to be near a barbecue grill or a loud radio. You want to walk down the beach and look for a good place to sit.

Let's Practice

Marita and Tranh are going to the beach. They want to swim, sunbathe, listen to music, and have a barbecue.

1. Make a list of the things Marita and Tranh should take to the beach. Work with a partner.

2. Exchange lists with another pair. Which items are the same on your lists? Which items are different? Add to your list if you forgot anything important.

3. There are three beaches near Marita and Tranh's city. Read the rules for each beach. Then decide which beach Marita and Tranh should go to. Work with your partner.

4. Read the beach rules again. Which beach should you go to

   a. if you want to take your dog?

   b. if you want to fish?

   c. if you want to go boating?

   d. if you are going to swim alone?

5. Which beach would you like to go to? Tell your partner why you would choose that beach.

OAK STREET BEACH
Rules

1. No barbecue grills
2. No boating
3. No pets
4. Beach open 6 A.M. to 10 P.M.

Let's Learn More

Read these paragraphs about beaches in the United States.

The United States has about ten thousand miles of **coastline**. The coastlines along the Atlantic and Pacific oceans and the Gulf of Mexico provide many miles of sandy beaches. The United States also has many beaches on the Great Lakes and on smaller **inland** lakes.

Americans who live near an ocean or lake may go to the beach quite often. Many other Americans enjoy spending their vacations at a beach. Some popular beach **resort** areas are in Hawaii, Florida, California, and Massachusetts.

Americans go to the beach to relax and to **socialize.** Many Americans participate in water sports such as swimming, surfing, snorkeling, scuba diving, boating, water-skiing, and fishing. Other popular beach activities include jogging and playing volleyball or Frisbee in the sand. Children enjoy building sand castles and playing in the sand and the water.

Another reason Americans go to the beach is to get a suntan. They may read, listen to music, or even sleep on their beach towels as they sunbathe. Most Americans think that tanned skin is very attractive and healthy-looking. However, scientists are learning how unhealthy the sun's rays can be. American newspaper and magazine articles tell readers that spending too much time in the sun can lead to skin cancer. Many Americans now protect themselves by wearing sunscreen, hats, and sunglasses. But many others still spend hours at the beach trying to get a great tan.

Vocabulary Check

Study these words and their meanings.

coastline   (n) the line where land and water (such as a lake or ocean) meet
inland   (adj) surrounded by land
resort   (n) a place that has hotels, shops, restaurants, and other attractions for vacationers
to socialize   (v) to talk and do things with people for fun

Now play "Categories." For each of these categories, write down all the words you can think of that have to do with the beach:

1. things to eat
2. things to play with
3. things to wear
4. places to go
5. ways to exercise

Read your words for each category out loud. The class will decide if the words belong in that category. You will receive one point for each correct word and subtract one point for each incorrect word. The student who has the most points for all five categories is the class expert on beaches!

Comprehension Check

Choose the best answer for each question.

1. What is the main point of the first paragraph?

   a. There are many lakes in the United States.
   b. There are many beaches in the United States.
   c. The United States is a big country.

2. Why do Americans go to the beach?

   a. to get a suntan   c. all of the above
   b. to relax and socialize

3. What is the main point of the last paragraph?

   a. Americans think that tanned skin is very attractive.
   b. Americans always use sunscreen, hats, and sunglasses to protect themselves from the sun.
   c. Most Americans know that the sun's rays can be dangerous, but they still think a suntan is attractive.

Extension Activity

In groups of four, make a television commercial for a new kind of sunscreen. Choose a name for your sunscreen and decide how you will convince people to buy it. Prepare and practice your commercial together. Then act it out for the rest of the class. If possible, videotape all the commercials and show them to another class. Have the students in that class vote on which sunscreen they would buy.

Chapter 18
Winter Sports and Activities

Warm-Up

❑ What are the winters like where you live?

❑ What winter sports and activities do you enjoy?

Words to Know

A. Here are the names of some things you can find in the winter. Look for them in the picture.

boots	Santa Claus	snow
coat	scarf	snowball
earmuffs	shovel	snowman
gloves	ski poles	snowmobile
hat	skis	snowplow
ice skates	sled	snowshoes
mittens	sleigh	toboggan

B. Here are some other words you can use to talk about winter sports and activities. Study these words and their meanings.

chair lift (n) a heavy rope with seats to carry people to the top of a mountain; a kind of ski lift

cross-country skiing (n) moving on skis across flat or slightly hilly land

downhill skiing (n) moving on skis down a mountain or steep hill

ice fishing (n) trying to catch fish through a hole cut in a frozen lake

ice hockey (n) a game played on ice by two teams of six players wearing ice skates

lift ticket (n) a card that permits a person to use a ski lift

skating rink (n) a place with smooth ice for ice-skating

ski lift (n) a heavy rope with seats or bars to carry people to the top of a ski slope

ski slope (n) part of a hill or mountain used for downhill skiing

C. Here are more words you can use to talk about the objects and activities in the picture.

avalanche	to fall down	to shovel
to be snowed in	hockey puck	to ski
to build a snowman	hockey stick	ski lodge
cast	to ice-skate	to sled
crutches	to play hockey	to throw
dogsled	polar bear	snowballs

Now complete these sentences with words from Lists A, B, and C. Change the form of a word if necessary.

1. A lot of snow, ice, and rock falling down the side of a mountain is called a/an _____ .

2. Enrique rode the _____ to the top of the mountain and then _____ down.

3. Some American children think that _____ travels in a _____ pulled by flying reindeer.

Understanding the Picture

1. Find someone in the picture who is doing each of these things.

   a. ice-skating
   b. ice fishing
   c. snowmobiling
   d. sledding
   e. skiing
   f. dogsledding
   g. snowshoeing
   h. building a snowman

2. Which of these kinds of transportation do you see in this picture?

   a. jeep
   b. airplane
   c. snowmobile
   d. car
   e. boat
   f. dogsled
   g. sleigh
   h. chair lift

3. Which item in each line is **not** in the picture?

a. hat, scarf, shorts, mittens, coat
b. fish, rabbit, dog, polar bear, reindeer
c. ski lodge, ski poles, ski boots, ski lift, ski jump
d. ice skater, hockey player, skier, fisherman, sailor

4. Many of the people in this picture are having problems. Which of these problems do you see?

a. A girl fell off a sled.
b. A fisherman caught a boot.
c. A skier is falling off the chair lift.
d. An ice skater fell down.
e. A man's car is snowed in.
f. A dog is chasing a hockey player.

What Do You See?

Study this part of the picture. Then answer the questions.

1. What is the polar bear doing? Is this believable? Why or why not?

2. What is the man with the brown hat doing?

3. What is the woman in the pink pants doing?

4. What is happening on the mountain?

5. What is the girl in the green coat doing?

What Are They Saying?

The woman in the pink pants is talking to the man on crutches. Practice their conversation with a partner.

MAN: Thank you for holding the door.

WOMAN: No problem. What happened to your leg?

MAN: I fell and broke my ankle while I was skiing yesterday.

WOMAN: That's too bad. Do you ski a lot?

MAN: No. This was my first time. Now my vacation is ruined! Why didn't I go to Florida?

WOMAN: I understand how you feel. Last year I broke my arm in a skiing accident. But here I am, skiing again!

MAN: You must love to ski.

WOMAN: I do. Don't worry—you will, too.

MAN: Can I buy you a cup of coffee?

WOMAN: Thanks, but not right now. My boyfriend is waiting for me by the chair lift.

Now work with your partner to change the conversation so that

- The man goes skiing every year.
- The man asks why he wasn't more careful.
- The woman broke her leg skiing last year.
- The woman will have a cup of coffee with the man.

Practice your new conversation together.

What Will Happen Next?

Answer these questions in small groups. Then compare your answers with those of the other groups.

1. What will happen to the people on the chair lift?

2. What will the man with the crutches do next?

3. What will happen to the skier in the green coat?

What Would You Say?

Act out this situation with a partner. Take turns playing parts A and B.

A. You are sitting by the fireplace in a ski lodge. You broke your leg skiing three days ago. Now you have nothing to do while your friends are skiing. You will be here for two more days.

B. You are tired from skiing all morning, so you go into the ski lodge. You see someone with a broken leg sitting by the fireplace. You start talking to him or her. Then you ask him or her to have lunch with you.

What Do You See?

Study this part of the picture. Then answer the questions.

1. What sports do you see in this part of the picture?

2. What is the boy with the red coat and yellow and red hat doing?

3. What is the dog doing?

4. What is the skater in the red and yellow suit doing?

5. What is the boy in the blue-green jacket doing?

What Are They Saying?

The boy in the blue-green jacket is talking to the girl with the pink earmuffs. Practice their conversation with a partner.

BOY: Are you okay?

GIRL: I think so.

BOY: Good. Come on, let me help you up.

GIRL: Oh Josh, I'll never be able to ice-skate!

BOY: Sure you will. You just need more practice.

GIRL: My ankles keep bending.

BOY: Maybe your skates are too loose. Let's get off the ice and I'll look at them.

GIRL: Why don't we go inside and get some hot chocolate?

BOY: That sounds like a good idea. Then you'll be ready for another skating lesson!

Work with your partner to change the conversation so that

- The girl's bottom hurts.
- The girl asks why ice-skating looks so easy.
- The boy says it *is* easy. She just needs more practice.
- The boy thinks the girl is tired. They should rest for a few minutes.
- The girl wants to get some lunch.

Practice your new conversation together.

What Will Happen Next?

Answer these questions in small groups. Then compare your answers with those of the other groups.

1. What will happen to the little girl who is ice-skating?

2. What will the hockey players do next?

3. What will the people on the snowmobiles do next?

What Would You Say?

Act out this situation in groups of three. Take turns playing parts A, B, and C.

A. You are at a skating rink with two friends. You are a good ice skater. You want to teach your friends to skate.

B. You are at a skating rink with two friends (A and C). You want to learn how to ice-skate. You fall down a lot, but you keep getting up and asking A for help.

C. You are at a skating rink with two friends. You try to skate a little, but after you fall down you don't want to try any more. You just want to watch your friends skate.

Let's Practice

Read this sign from the Snowflake Winter Sports Park. Then answer the questions with a partner.

SNOWFLAKE WINTER SPORTS PARK

Open 9 A.M. to 7 P.M. daily
between November 1 and March 1.

Parking: FREE
Daily Admission: Adults $10.00 • Children (under 10) $5.00
Two-Day Admission: Adults $15.00 • Children (under 10) $8.00
Season Pass: Adults $50.00 • Children (under 10) $25.00

Equipment Rental

Sleds and Ice Skates
FREE with paid admission.

Snowmobiles
$1.50 per hour/ $4.00 per half day/ $6.00 per full day

Skis, Ski Poles, and Boots
$1.00 per hour/ $2.50 per half day/ $4.00 per full day

Lift Tickets: Adults $5.00 per day
Children (under 10) $2.00 per day
❄ Free with Season Pass ❄

Understanding the Sign

1. How much does it cost to park your car at the Snowflake Winter Sports Park?

2. How much does it cost to enter the park?

3. What equipment can you use for free at the park? What equipment must you pay to use?

4. How much does it cost to rent a snowmobile for an hour?

5. How much does it cost to use the ski lift?

6. In what months can you go to the Snowflake Winter Sports Park?

7. What hours is the park open?

Using the Information

1. You, your mother, and your nine-year-old brother want to spend the day skiing at the Snowflake Winter Sports Park. What will this cost?

2. You and a friend want to spend the day snowmobiling at the Snowflake Winter Sports Park. What will this cost?

3. You and your parents want to spend two days skiing at the Snowflake Winter Sports Park. You have your own skis, ski poles, and boots. How much money will you have to pay?

4. You live close to the Snowflake Winter Sports Park. You plan to go sledding and ice-skating at the park eight times this winter. Will it be cheaper for you to buy a season pass, pay the daily admission prices, or pay the two-day admission prices?

Let's Learn More

Read these paragraphs about winter sports and activities in the United States.

Winter sports and activities are very popular in the United States. People in many parts of the country enjoy ice-skating, sledding, snowmobiling, and cross-country skiing whenever there is enough snow or ice on the ground. Downhill skiing is most common in the Rocky Mountains and Sierra Nevada Mountains in the West, and in the Appalachian Mountains in the northeastern United States. These areas have many **ski resorts** where Americans from all over the country go to ski.

Most ski resorts have slopes (and lessons) for beginning, intermediate, and advanced skiers. Ski lifts carry people to the top of each slope. Other activities, such as ice-skating, sledding, cross-country skiing, and indoor swimming are usually available. Some ski resorts are very expensive, while others offer children's programs and cheaper prices for families.

Some winter sports, such as ice hockey, skating, and skiing, are played by both **amateurs** and **professionals.** For example, professional ice hockey teams from the United States and Canada **compete** in the National Hockey League. However, to most Americans, the most exciting winter sports competition is the Winter Olympics, held every four years. Amateur skaters, skiers, and other **athletes** from all over the world spend years practicing for the chance to compete in the Olympics and win a gold, silver, or bronze **medal** for their country.

Vocabulary Check

Study these words and their meanings.

amateur   (n) a person who does something for fun, not for money; someone who is not a professional
athlete   (n) someone who is good at sports
to compete   (v) to be in a contest or race
medal   (n) a prize that looks like a big coin
professional   (n) a person who is paid to do something; someone who is not an amateur
ski resort   (n) a place that has ski slopes and a ski lodge

Now find words in the reading that mean the opposite of these words and phrases.

1. bottom
2. professional
3. cheap
4. dull; boring
5. lose
6. people who are not good at sports
7. more expensive
8. amateur
9. East
10. outdoor

Comprehension Check

Decide whether each sentence is true or false. If a sentence is false, change it to make it true.

1. Very few Americans enjoy winter sports and activities.

2. Professional athletes compete in the Olympics every year.

3. Many Americans go downhill skiing in the Rocky Mountains.

4. Athletes can win gold, silver, or copper medals in the Winter Olympics.

5. Most ski resorts have places for beginning, intermediate, and advanced skiers to ski.

Extension Activity

With your class, make a list of winter sports and activities on the board. Then find out how many students in your class ever played each sport or activity. Which one did (do) the most students play? Which one did (do) the fewest students play? Is there a sport or activity that everyone (or no one) in the class ever played?

"Interview" a partner about his or her favorite winter sport or activity. Ask questions about when and where your partner plays, whom he plays with, and when and where he learned to play. Then let your partner interview you. Write a paragraph about your partner and his or her favorite winter sport or activity. Don't use your partner's name in your paragraph. Don't write your name on your paper.

Give your paragraph to your teacher. Then your teacher will give every student someone else's paragraph to read. Take turns reading the paragraphs to the class. See if the class can guess who each paragraph is about.

Chapter 19

At an Outdoor Concert

Warm-Up

❑ What kind(s) of music do you like?

❑ Did you ever go to an outdoor concert? If so, where was it? What kind of music did you hear?

Words to Know

A. Here are the names of some things you can find at an outdoor concert. Look for them in the picture.

amplifier	guitar	musician
blanket	guitarist	picnic basket
cooler	keyboard	security guard
drummer	lawn chair	speaker
drums	microphone	stage

B. Here are some other words you can use to talk about an outdoor concert. Study these words and their meanings.

to attend (v) to go to

audience (n) people who are attending a performance

blues (n) a kind of music that is slow and sad, developed from African-American work songs and religious music

classical music (n) the traditional European style of music, including operas and symphonies

country and western music (n) a kind of music that developed in the United States from western cowboy songs and southern folk songs

fan (n) someone who likes a sport or a performer a lot

gospel music (n) a kind of religious music sung in a blues style, developed by African-Americans

jazz (n) a kind of music with special rhythms that developed from blues music

performance (n) a concert, play, or other program

performer (n) someone who sings, acts, or does something else in front of an audience

picnic (n) a meal that you eat outside

rock and roll (n) also called rock; a kind of popular music that has a heavy beat

souvenir (n) an object that helps you remember something

technician (n) someone who knows a lot about a certain kind of equipment or machinery

C. Here are more words you can use to talk about the objects and activities in the picture.

barbecue grill	Mohawk haircut
cape	portable rest rooms
to clap	tattoo
Frisbee	ticket booth
litter	to wait in line

Now complete these sentences with words from Lists A and B. Change the form of a word if necessary.

1. Mary is a big _____ of the Detroit Lions. She _____ all their games.

2. Cindy bought a lot of _____ when she visited New York.

3. If you go to an outdoor concert, take a _____ or a _____ to sit on.

Understanding the Picture

1. What group is performing at this concert?

2. What kind of music does this group play?

3. Which of these things can you buy at this concert?

   a. a Frisbee   e. pizza
   b. a ticket   f. ice cream
   c. a lawn chair   g. a T-shirt
   d. a hot dog   h. a barbecue grill

4. Which of these things are the fans doing to show how much they like the Rock Lizards?

a. holding a sign
b. clapping
c. yelling
d. eating
e. dressing like the performers
f. barbecuing
g. waving
h. leaving

5. Some of the people in the audience are not watching the concert. Find someone who is doing each of these things.

a. buying food
b. going to the rest room
c. playing Frisbee
d. talking to a friend
e. standing in line
f. eating
g. carrying food and drinks
h. unfolding a blanket

What Do You See?

Study this part of the picture. Then answer the questions.

1. What is the performer in the flowered shirt doing?

2. What are the people in the audience doing?

3. What are the security guards doing?

4. What is the performer with the cape doing?

5. Who are the two men by the speaker? What are they doing?

What Are They Saying?

One of the security guards is talking to the boy in the white T-shirt and the girl in the blue shirt. Practice their conversation in groups of three.

SECURITY GUARD: May I see your ticket, please?

BOY: Sure. Just a minute. *(pause)* Here it is.

SECURITY GUARD: This ticket is for Section B. You're in Section A.

BOY: Where is Section B?

SECURITY GUARD: Back there, behind the ropes.

BOY: But I won't be able to see very well back there.

SECURITY GUARD: I'm sorry, but your ticket is for Section B. You'll have to move back.
(to girl) Excuse me. May I see your ticket, please?

GIRL: What's the problem?

SECURITY GUARD: There's no problem. I'm just checking everyone's tickets.

GIRL: Oh. Here it is.

SECURITY GUARD: Okay. Thank you. Enjoy the concert.

Now work with your partner to change the conversation so that

- The boy says he won't be able to hear very well in Section B.
- The security guard says the music is so loud you can hear it in the parking lot.
- The girl can't hear the security guard's question.
- The security guard tells her what he wants again, more loudly.

Practice your new conversation together.

What Will Happen Next?

Answer these questions in small groups. Then compare your answers with those of the other groups.

1. What will the two men by the speaker do next?

2. What will happen to the fans who are holding the sign?

3. What will the TV cameraman do next?

What Would You Say?

Act out this situation with a partner. Take turns playing parts A and B.

A. You and a friend are going to buy tickets for the Rock Lizards concert. You want to buy tickets for Section A. Your friend wants to buy tickets for Section B. You try to convince your friend that Section A is better.

B. You and a friend are going to buy tickets for the Rock Lizards concert. You want to buy tickets for Section B. Your friend wants to buy tickets for Section A. You try to convince your friend that Section B is better.

What Do You See?

Study this part of the picture. Then answer the questions.

1. What is the dog doing?

2. What is the man in the blue shorts doing?

3. What are the people sitting on?

4. What is behind the ticket booth?

5. What is the girl in the purple shirt and pink pants doing?

What Are They Saying?

The girls in the lawn chairs are talking about the concert. Practice their conversation with a partner.

GIRL 1: Isn't this a great concert?

GIRL 2: It sure is! I can't believe you never went to a Rock Lizards concert before.

GIRL 1: I don't go to many concerts. They're so expensive.

GIRL 2: That's true. But I never miss a Rock Lizards concert! Last year I saw them perform five times.

GIRL 1: Wow! Listen—this sounds like a new song.

GIRL 2: It is. It's on their new album, "Live Lizards." I just bought it yesterday.

GIRL 1: Oh. I didn't know they had a new album.

GIRL 2: Guess what? I'm going to the Rock Lizards concert in Springfield tomorrow night!

GIRL 1: You are? That's a three-hour drive!

GIRL 2: I know, but I don't care. I love the Rock Lizards!

Now work with your partner to change the conversation so that

- Girl 1 asks Girl 2 if she likes the concert.
- This isn't a new song. It's on the Rock Lizards' third album.
- Girl 1 doesn't have that album.
- Springfield is sixty miles away.

Practice your new conversation together.

What Will Happen Next?

Answer these questions in small groups. Then compare your answers with those of the other groups.

1. What will the man in the blue shorts do next?

2. What will happen to the dog?

3. What will the woman holding the lawn chair and cooler do next?

What Would You Say?

Act out this situation in groups of three. Take turns playing parts A, B, and C.

A. You are talking to two friends at school. You went to a Five Sisters rock concert last night. You like the group's music, and you enjoyed the concert.

B. You are talking to two friends at school. You went to the Five Sisters rock concert last night. You thought it was too noisy and hot.

C. You are talking to two friends at school. You didn't go to the Five Sisters rock concert last night. You don't like the Five Sisters.

Let's Practice

You can buy many souvenirs at a Rock Lizards concert.
Look at this list of souvenirs. Then answer the questions with a partner.

ROCK LIZARDS
SOUVENIRS

BUTTONS: $1.50   BUMPER STICKERS: $8.00
POSTERS: $5.00   TOUR JACKETS: $35.00
FRISBEES: $5.00   HATS: SOLD OUT
T-SHIRTS: Adult S, M, L, XL $15.00
                  Child S, M, L $10.00
SWEATSHIRTS: Adult S, M, L, XL $25.00

OFFICIAL CONCERT PROGRAM $5.00

1. Which of the souvenirs can you put on a wall?

2. Which of the souvenirs can you put on a car?

3. Which of the souvenirs can you play with?

4. Which of the souvenirs can you wear?

5. Which of the souvenirs is available in children's sizes?

6. Which souvenir is the most expensive?

7. Which souvenir is the cheapest?

8. Which souvenir is not available today?

9. Which is more expensive, a bumper sticker or a Frisbee?

10. Which is more expensive, an adult's T-shirt or a sweatshirt?

11. You have five dollars to spend on a souvenir. What can you buy?

12. You are buying a sweatshirt and a concert program. How much will this cost?

13. You are buying a button and a poster. How much will this cost?

14. You are buying two adult T-shirts and a child's T-shirt. How much will this cost?

15. You are buying a tour jacket and a Frisbee. How much will this cost?

Let's Learn More

Read these paragraphs about outdoor concerts in the United States.

Outdoor concerts are a popular part of summer in the United States. People of all ages enjoy listening to music outside on a warm evening, often while sitting in lawn chairs or on blankets on the grass. Many kinds of outdoor concerts take place all over the United States. Each **setting** and each kind of music **appeals to** different people.

Some outdoor concerts take place in **open-air** theaters or **bandstands** in city parks. **Local** bands, singing groups, and orchestras perform in these free concerts. People of all ages, including whole families, often attend.

Other outdoor concerts are part of special **festivals** in parks or on city streets. Many groups, playing different kinds of music, may perform all day long on bandstands built especially for the festival. These concerts are usually free to anyone attending the festival.

Another kind of outdoor concert takes place at big open-air theaters that are usually found near large cities. Famous rock groups and other performers travel all over the country to play concerts in theaters like these. Every year, thousands of Americans pay to attend this kind of concert. Most of the concerts are performed by rock groups and attended by young people. However, some open-air theaters present other kinds of concerts, such as classical or country and western, that are attended by different groups of people.

Vocabulary Check

Study these words and their meanings.

to appeal to   (v) to interest, to attract
bandstand   (n) a covered stage where musical groups can perform outdoors
festival   (n) a special celebration that often includes dancing, music, and food
local   (adj) nearby; from a certain place
open-air   (adj) outdoor
setting   (n) the time and place in which something happens

Now find words in the reading that have these meanings.

1. go to
2. outdoor
3. not costing any money
4. very well-known
5. celebrations
6. attracts
7. liked by most people
8. musical performances

Comprehension Check

Choose the best word or phrase to complete each sentence.

1. Many people take _____ to an outdoor concert. (blankets and lawn chairs, bands and orchestras)

2. Most young Americans like to attend _____ concerts. (classical, rock)

3. Outdoor concerts often take place in _____ . (settings, open-air theaters)

4. Some city parks have _____ for outdoor concerts. (festivals, bandstands)

5. Some outdoor concerts are expensive to attend, while others are _____ . (famous, free)

Extension Activity

Take a survey to find out which American singers and musical groups are your class's favorites. Then bring a song from the most popular performer to play in class. (Let your teacher help decide which song to use.) Listen carefully to the words. Write them on the board and talk about what they mean. Listen to the song a few more times and practice singing it together. Talk about why you think this song is so popular. What does each student like and/or dislike about it?

Chapter 20
At an Amusement Park
Warm-Up

❑ What is an amusement park? Why do people go to amusement parks?

❑ Did you ever go to an amusement park? If so, what did you do there?

Words to Know

A. Here are the names of some things you can find at an amusement park. Look for them in the picture.

balloon	hot dog	roller coaster
camera	merry-go-round	ticket booth
clown	picnic table	train
Ferris wheel		

B. Here are some other words you can use to talk about an amusement park. Study these words and their meanings.

to attract (v) to make someone want to come nearer
attraction (n) something that attracts or interests people
to entertain (v) to amuse or interest
entertainment (n) something that interests or amuses
general store (n) an old-fashioned store that sells many different things, including food and clothing
horror (n) strong, painful fear or shock
picnic (n) a meal to eat outside
ride (n) something to ride on for fun, such as a merry-go-round or a Ferris wheel
scared (adj) full of fear; frightened; afraid
scary (adj) frightening; causing fear
tunnel (n) an underground road

C. Here are more words you can use to talk about the picture. Look for examples of these objects and activities in the picture.

bucket	gun	to spill
to cover one's eyes	to hug	squirrel
cowboy	pool	teddy bear
engineer	porpoise	turban
fish	to scream	to watch
to fly off	to shoot	to wave

Now complete these sentences with words from Lists A, B, and C. Change the form of a word if necessary.

1. Pam _____ and _____ while her little brother rode on the merry-go-round.

2. A _____ looks like a big wheel with seats.

3. An _____ drives a train.

4. Joel and Lisa went on all the _____ at the amusement park.

Understanding the Picture

1. Which of these rides do you see at this amusement park?

   a. Ferris wheel
   b. swing set
   c. merry-go-round
   d. water slide
   e. train
   f. bicycle
   g. roller coaster
   h. tunnel of horror

2. There are many things to do at this amusement park. Find someone who is doing each of these things.

   a. buying tickets
   b. watching a gunfight
   c. taking a picture
   d. eating lunch
   e. watching a porpoise show
   f. getting a balloon
   g. buying hot dogs
   h. waving to a child

3. There are many people working at this amusement park. Which of these jobs are they doing?

a. selling tickets
b. going on rides
c. feeding the porpoise
d. driving the train
e. feeding the birds
f. giving away balloons
g. riding horses
h. pretending to be cowboys

4. Which item in each line is **not** in the picture?

a. cowboy, engineer, astronaut, clown
b. dog, porpoise, squirrel, cat
c. french fries, popcorn, sandwich, hot dog
d. turban, helmet, cowboy hat, baseball cap

What Do You See?

Study this part of the picture. Then answer the questions.

1. What is happening at the picnic tables?

2. What is the woman in the yellow dress doing?

3. What is the porpoise doing?

4. What is the man with the red hat doing?

5. What rides do you see in this part of the picture?

What Are They Saying?

The woman on the train is talking to her little boy. Practice their conversation with a partner.

WOMAN: Look, Tommy! There's the merry-go-round.

BOY: And the roller coaster! Can we ride on that?

WOMAN: I guess we can. If you really want to.

BOY: Great! Can we go on the Ferris wheel, too?

WOMAN: I guess so. Do you want to see the porpoise show?

BOY: If we have time. I mostly want to go on the rides.

WOMAN: Why don't we try the merry-go-round first?

BOY: Oh, Mom. Merry-go-rounds are for babies!

WOMAN: They are? Then I'm the biggest baby here.

Now work with your partner to change the conversation so that

- Tommy wants to ride on the Ferris wheel and go in the Tunnel of Horror.
- Tommy's mother doesn't think they should go in the Tunnel of Horror.
- Tommy's mother asks if he wants to get a hot dog or some popcorn.

Practice your new conversation together.

What Will Happen Next?

Answer these questions in small groups. Then compare your answers with those of the other groups.

1. What will the people who went in the Tunnel of Horror do next?

2. What will the woman in the yellow dress do next?

3. What will the porpoise do next?

What Would You Say?

Act out this situation with a partner. Take turns playing parts A and B.

A. You are at an amusement park with a friend. You want to go on all the scary rides. You want your friend to go on the scary rides with you.

B. You are at an amusement park with a friend. You don't want to go on any scary rides. You want to see some shows and go on some rides that aren't scary. You want your friend to do these things with you.

What Do You See?

Study this part of the picture. Then answer the questions.

1. What is the red-haired girl on the merry-go-round doing?

2. What is the clown doing?

3. What is the woman with the purple hat doing?

4. What is happening on the roller coaster?

5. What is the girl in the yellow shirt doing?

What Are They Saying?

The woman with the purple hat is talking to the employee at the ticket booth. Practice their conversation with a partner.

WOMAN: Hi. How much are the tickets?

EMPLOYEE: They're a dollar each, or fifteen for ten dollars.

WOMAN: How many tickets does each ride cost?

EMPLOYEE: Some cost two tickets, and some cost one.

WOMAN: Do children and adults pay the same price?

EMPLOYEE: Yes, they do.

WOMAN: I guess I'll buy fifteen tickets.

EMPLOYEE: Okay. That will be ten dollars. (*pause*) Here are your tickets. Have fun!

WOMAN: Thanks. We will!

Now work with your partner to change the conversation so that

- The tickets are fifty cents each, or twelve for five dollars.
- Some rides cost three tickets, and some cost two.
- The woman asks which rides cost three tickets.
- The woman will buy twenty-four tickets.

Practice your new conversation together.

What Will Happen Next?

Answer these questions in small groups. Then compare your answers with those of the other groups.

1. What will happen to the people on the roller coaster?

2. What will the man in the black shirt do next?

3. What will the girl in the yellow shirt and the boy in the red shirt do next?

What Would You Say?

Act out this situation in groups of three. Take turns playing parts A, B, and C.

A. You are at an amusement park with your child. You are buying tickets for the rides. You don't want to spend a lot of money.

B. You are at an amusement park with your parent. You want to go on all the rides. You want your parent to buy a lot of tickets.

C. You are an employee at an amusement park ticket booth. You are helping A decide how many tickets to buy.

Let's Practice

Look at this map of the Magic Moments amusement park.

Now work with a partner to answer these questions.

Understanding the Map

1. What kinds of food can you buy at Magic Moments?

2. What other things can you buy at Magic Moments?

3. Where can little children have fun at Magic Moments?

4. Which ride lets you see the whole amusement park?

5. Where can you go to see a show at Magic Moments?

6. Which ride is in the middle of the amusement park?

Following the Map

1. You are at the entrance. You want to ride on the Flash Flood. Should you take the path to the left or to the right?

2. You are at the entrance. You want to play video games. Should you take the path to the left or to the right?

3. You are at the balloon stand. You want to ride on the Ax. Should you walk east or west on the path?

4. You are at the Magical Merry-Go-Round. You want to go to Bob's Burger Barn. Should you take the path to the east or to the west?

Making Choices

With your partner, ask and answer these questions. Give reasons for each of your answers.

1. Would you ride on the cable cars at Magic Moments?

2. Would you ride on the Whipper-Snapper at Magic Moments?

3. Would you ride on the Flash Flood at Magic Moments?

4. Would you go to the Porpoise Show at Magic Moments?

5. Would you play video games at Magic Moments?

6. Where would you like to eat at Magic Moments?

7. What would you like to buy at Magic Moments?

8. If you could do just three things at Magic Moments, what would you do?

Let's Learn More

Read these paragraphs about U.S. amusement parks.

Amusement parks are places to have fun. Most amusement parks offer a variety of rides and shows for people to enjoy. More than 170 million people visit amusement parks every year in the United States. People usually stay for several hours or all day when they go to an amusement park.

The first amusement parks in the United States were built in the 1800s. For many years, the most famous amusement parks in the world were on Coney Island, a small **peninsula** on the Atlantic Coast in Brooklyn, New York. In the 1820s, Coney Island was a popular **seaside resort** for **wealthy** people. In the late 1800s, it became popular with **working-class** people, too. Several amusement parks—and the world's first roller coaster—were built on the peninsula in the late 1800s and early 1900s. Today, ten million people a year still visit Coney Island, although many of its attractions are now gone.

U.S. amusement parks began to change in the mid-1900s. Before that time, they were usually found in cities. Now they are mostly found in the **suburbs.** Today, most U.S. amusement parks are called "theme parks." Their rides, shows, restaurants, and shops follow historical or cultural **themes.** At most U.S. theme parks, people do not have to pay for each ride or show. They pay only to enter the park. Then they can see the shows and go on the rides as many times as they want to in one day. Of course, they must pay for any food or souvenirs they buy in the park.

Vocabulary Check

Study these words and their meanings.

peninsula   (n) a piece of land that sticks out into the water

seaside resort   (n) a place by an ocean that has hotels, shops, restaurants, and beaches to attract vacationers

suburb   (n) a small town or community on the edge of a big city

theme   (n) a topic or subject

wealthy   (adj) having a lot of money; rich

working-class   (adj) having to do with people who must work for the money they need to live

Now play "Categories." For each of these categories, write down all the words you can think of that have to do with amusement parks:

1. food
2. rides
3. entertainment
4. places
5. money

Read your words for each category out loud. The class will decide if the words belong in that category. You will receive one point for each correct word and subtract one point for each incorrect word. The student who has the most points for all five categories is the class expert on amusement parks!

Comprehension Check

Answer each question in a complete sentence.

1. How many people go to amusement parks in the United States?

2. Where is Coney Island?

3. Where are most U.S. amusement parks?

4. What are most U.S. amusement parks called today?

5. What do people do at amusement parks?

Extension Activity

In groups of three or four, pretend to be the owners of Magic Moments amusement park. You want to attract more people to your park. Choose an age group to work on (young children, teenagers, adults, or senior citizens). Talk about what people of this age group like to do. What can you do to attract more people of this age to your park? Make a list of ideas (for example, adding a new kind of ride or show). Talk about the ideas, and choose the three ideas you think are the best.

Tell the rest of the class about your group's ideas for attracting more people to Magic Moments. Explain why you think your ideas will work. Let the class vote on the best idea for attracting each age group.

Index of Vocabulary

Below is an alphabetical listing of the words and phrases included in the **Words to Know** and **Vocabulary Check** sections of the text. The numbers indicate the pages on which the words are listed. Each word is defined on the indicated page and/or illustrated in the corresponding chapter illustration.

horse   16
hose   54
hot dog   124
hotel   10
hubcap   62
to hug   124
hurdle   94
to hurry   54

I

ice fishing   112
ice hockey   112
ice machine   86
to ice-skate   112
ice skates   112
illegal   10
immigrant   4
to immigrate   4
to improve   41
to increase   41
Indian corn   22
Indians   22
industrialized   15
inexpensive   53
information booth   68, 74, 80
inland   111
insecticide   21
to inspect   80
inspection   9
to insure   35
to insure an item   36
intercity   73, 79
interest   30
intersection   10
investment   35
island   4

J

jack   62
jazz   100, 118
jeep   62
to jog   100

K

kayak   4
keyboard   118
kite   100

L

ladder   54
ladder truck   54
to land   80
laundromat   86
lawn chair   100, 118
to lay an egg   16
to lead   94
leaf   100
leash   100
letter   36
lettuce   42
license plate   62
to lick   22, 36
lifeguard   106
life preserver   106
lift ticket   112
limousine   10, 62
litter   118
livestock   16
loan   30
lobster   42
local   123
locker   68, 94
locker room   94
long jump   94
lost and found department   68
loudspeaker   68, 74
luggage   68, 74, 80
luggage cart   74, 80
luggage tag   80

M

mail carrier   36
mail slot   36
to make a touchdown   94
manufacturer   47
mascot   94
meal   48
meat counter   42
mechanic   62, 80
medal   117
meet   94
to meet   80
megaphone   4, 54
memorial   4
menu   48
to merge   73